Michael Crichton

Titles in the People in the News series include:

PEOPLE
IN THE NEWS

Michael Crichton

by Nathan Aaseng

LUCENT BOOKS
SAN DIEGO, CALIFORNIA

THOMSON
———✦———™
GALE

Detroit • New York • San Diego • San Francisco
Boston • New Haven, Conn. • Waterville, Maine
London • Munich

Library of Congress Cataloging-in-Publication Data

Aaseng, Nathan.
    Michael Crichton / by Nathan Aaseng.
        p. cm. — (People in the news)
Includes bibliographical references and index.
Summary: Profiles the life of Michael Crichton, revealing how his childhood interests helped him to become a best-selling author of technothriller books and films, as well as creator of the television series, ER.
    ISBN 1-59018-019-4 (hardback : alk. paper)
    1. Crichton, Michael, 1942– —Juvenile literature. 2. Novelists, American—20th century—Biography—Juvenile literature. 3. Science fiction—Authorship—Juvenile literature. [1. Crichton, Michael, 1942– 2. Authors, American.] I. Title. II. People in the news (San Diego, Calif.)
    PS3553.R48 Z5 2002
    813'.54—dc21

2001005526

Copyright © 2002 by Lucent Books,
an imprint of The Gale Group
10911 Technology Place, San Diego, CA 92127
Printed in the U.S.A.

Table of Contents

Foreword

FAME AND CELEBRITY are alluring. People are drawn to those who walk in fame's spotlight, whether they are known for great accomplishments or for notorious deeds. The lives of the famous pique public interest and attract attention, perhaps because their experiences seem in some ways so different from, yet in other ways so similar to, our own.

Newspapers, magazines, and television regularly capitalize on this fascination with celebrity by running profiles of famous people. For example, television programs such as *Entertainment Tonight* devote all of their programming to stories about entertainment and entertainers. Magazines such as *People* fill their pages with stories of the private lives of famous people. Even newspapers, newsmagazines, and television news frequently delve into the lives of well-known personalities. Despite the number of articles and programs, few provide more than a superficial glimpse at their subjects.

Lucent's People in the News series offers young readers a deeper look into the lives of today's newsmakers, the influences that have shaped them, and the impact they have had in their fields of endeavor and on other people's lives. The subjects of the series hail from many disciplines and walks of life. They include authors, musicians, athletes, political leaders, entertainers, entrepreneurs, and others who have made a mark on modern life and who, in many cases, will continue to do so for years to come.

These biographies are more than factual chronicles. Each book emphasizes the contributions, accomplishments, or deeds that have brought fame or notoriety to the individual and shows how that person has influenced modern life. Authors portray their subjects in a realistic, unsentimental light. For example, Bill Gates—the cofounder and chief executive officer of the software giant Microsoft—has been instrumental in making personal computers the most vital tool of the modern age. Few dispute his business savvy, his perseverance, or his technical expertise, yet critics say he is ruthless in his dealings with competitors and driven more by his desire to maintain Microsoft's dominance in the computer industry than by an interest in furthering technology.

In these books, young readers will encounter inspiring stories about real people who achieved success despite enormous obstacles. Oprah Winfrey—the most powerful, most watched, and wealthiest woman on television today—spent the first six years of her life in the care of her grandparents while her unwed mother sought work and a better life elsewhere. Her adolescence was colored by promiscuity, pregnancy at age fourteen, rape, and sexual abuse.

Each author documents and supports his or her work with an array of primary and secondary source quotations taken from diaries, letters, speeches, and interviews. All quotes are footnoted to show readers exactly how and where biographers derive their information and provide guidance for further research. The quotations enliven the text by giving readers eyewitness views of the life and accomplishments of each person covered in the People in the News series.

In addition, each book in the series includes photographs, annotated bibliographies, timelines, and comprehensive indexes. For both the casual reader and the student researcher, the People in the News series offers insight into the lives of today's newsmakers—people who shape the way we live, work, and play in the modern age.

Creator of the Technothriller

F OR MOST OF the twentieth century, science fiction attracted a relatively small but passionate audience of readers who enjoyed imagining the effects of scientific and technological advances on human society. However, the majority of readers, who found technology and science confusing and tedious, turned away.

Michael Crichton has changed all that. More than any other writer, Crichton has been able to break down those intimidating barriers that divide the scientific world from the general public. He has done so by conjuring up some of the most fascinating, terrifying, and thought-provoking situations that can result from scientific and technological discoveries.

According to Theodore Sturgeon, writing in the *New York Times Book Review,* "Crichton's beat is in the interface between fact and invention, certainty and possibility, the established and the extrapolated."[1] In Crichton's world, a pack of velociraptors cloned from preserved mosquito DNA break into a barricaded building and stalk the terrified inhabitants. Deadly bacteria from outer space, for which there is no earthly immunity, threaten to annihilate the entire human race. A computerized medical device implanted to save the life of an accident victim goes haywire, turning the patient into a maniacal killer. A mysterious sphere lying at the bottom of the ocean floor transforms a research expedition into a nightmare. A gorilla who can speak in sign language is all that stands between a group of explorers and a murderous band of apes.

"Footnotes in His Fiction"

Such a legacy of spellbinding tales would have, in itself, distinguished Crichton from the pack of modern fiction writers. But Crichton is more than an entertainer; he is a compulsive teacher. Into each of his suspenseful stories, Crichton packs clear and readable explanations of some of the most advanced topics in science and technology. Lured into the story by Crichton's intriguing and fast-paced plot, millions of readers with no previous interest in such complex subjects as the history and workings of computers, the techniques of genetic engineering, the principles of aerodynamics, the functions of the nervous and circulatory systems of dinosaurs, and the mind-boggling mathematical significance of the chaos theory come away from Crichton's books with at least a basic understanding of those topics. His research and the documentation of his subjects is so thorough that Frank Marshall, who directed a movie based on a Crichton story, comments, "He's the only writer I know who has footnotes in his fiction."[2] According to *Current Biography,*

Crichton is credited with creating the technothriller, a literary genre that combines technical topics with intriguing plots.

Crichton has a rare gift of folding highly technical material into "works whose suspenseful plots are somehow never overwhelmed by the scientific data and 'technospeak.'"[3]

Although Crichton revels in technological detail, his interest in educating the public extends far beyond a mountain of facts. What the author is really concerned about are ideas, issues, and disturbing trends that he sees threatening the modern world, and he is not shy about using his status as a best-selling author to express his strongly held opinions. "Crichton uses science as the stuff for writing about a different genre," observes Nicholas Wade in the *New York Times Magazine*. "At heart, he's a moralist. The hostile forces he portrays are not implacable aliens; they emanate from the failings he sees in ourselves."[4]

Crichton's literary skill, ability to explain technical material to nonexperts, and boldness in tackling moral issues led him to create a new genre of fiction known as the technothriller. The technothriller takes a difficult moral issue that arises from technology, provides a vast number of facts to educate the reader about the subject, and packages it in a story filled with suspense and nonstop action. As Ron Givens explains in *Newsweek,* what Crichton does best is "giv[e] us suspense for our nerve endings and enough scientific speculation to keep our brains working at the same time."[5]

Not everyone admires the literary form of the technothriller or Crichton's style of writing it. Such books are primarily concerned with plot at the expense of characters. Throughout his career, Crichton has been criticized for populating his books with colorless, empty beings with no more personality than robots. Typical of the complaints was Daniel Mendelsohn's observation in the *New York Times Book Review* that "Crichton's lack of curiosity about humans and their inner motivations limits him even as a science-fiction writer."[6] To some, the author seems to find machines more fascinating than people.

Another criticism of Crichton concerns his close ties with the motion picture industry. Crichton learned early in his career the rewards of writing books that can easily be adapted to the more financially rewarding media of motion pictures. He has shown an uncanny ability to deliver what consumers in the movie in-dustry want. As a result, say critics, he sometimes appears to be writing not a novel but a storyboard for a movie, focusing on ac-tion scenes at the expense of both plot and character. They ques-tion whether Crichton is concerned with writing a quality book or just making a buck. Nonetheless, even his most severe critics agree that Crichton has explored more themes and more provocative issues in society and has opened up more bewilder-ing worlds of science to the average reader than any other pop-ular writer alive.

Piles of Books

Crichton has achieved success with the technothriller because he is a man of rare intelligence who quickly masters the basics of all man-ner of subjects and occupations. He is not only a writer but a trained medical doctor, anthropologist, motion picture director, software de-signer, and video game creator. Along with being a quick study, Crichton is a man of insatiable curiosity about the world. He has traveled throughout the world in a vast array of cultures, and he reads incessantly.

> "All the bedrooms are stacked (with books)," Crichton has admitted. "There are books piled in the garage, and there are books in boxes in the basement. The paperbacks are yel-low and cracked, but I won't give them up. I can't—I an-notate as I read. At one point I calculated that half the weight and value of what we own is books."[7]

The vast scope of his interests have lured him out of the world of science and technology into other controversial subjects, includ-ing abortion, sexual harassment, and economic warfare.

Crichton's most useful gift lies in his ability to describe the world he sees in clear, accurate, and understandable terms. What he sees most often are challenges and dangers at the edge of scien-tific progress. Hundreds of millions of people throughout the world have been exposed to those hair-raising possibilities, pulled along on the wild, breakneck rides designed for them by the master of the technothriller.

Chapter 1

Childhood Dreams

JOHN MICHAEL CRICHTON's world began on October 23, 1942, in Chicago, Illinois, where he was the first child of John Henderson Crichton and Zula Crichton. Since he shared the same first name as his father, he was called by his middle name. The last name, which is of Scottish descent, rhymes with *frighten*.

John Henderson was a journalist who discovered an opportunity to make more money using his writing skills in the advertising world. Shortly after Michael was born, John Henderson moved the family to Roslyn, a Long Island suburb of New York, where he began his new career. He did well enough at it that he worked his way to executive editor of *Advertising Age* magazine and eventually served as president of the American Association of Advertising Agencies.

Zula Crichton concentrated her efforts as a homemaker for a family that grew to include four children. From an early age, Michael displayed an independent nature. Zula later quipped that, when it came to raising her independent-minded oldest son, "I just [got] out of his way."[8] However, she did take an active role in exposing her children to a wide variety of cultural events. As the children grew older, Zula Crichton regularly took them to concerts, plays, museums, and movies.

Both parents encouraged the children to develop their own interests and tastes. Michael Crichton remembers that as a child he was "always interested in lots of things. It was an idea in my family that it was good to have an interest in many diverse things—that you didn't have to have a scheme where it all fit together."[9] Among those diverse interests were science, reading, and writing.

Like many youngsters, Crichton's dreams about a future career shifted from time to time. He remembers writing being one of these earliest ambitions in life, dating back almost to when he first learned to read and write. Crichton particularly remembers an assignment in third grade in which the students were asked to write a puppet show. Although most of his classmates came up with brief skits, young Michael found he could not stop until he had finished a complex nine-page play. His interests quickly shifted to the scientific world, however. As he recalls, "At 10, I wanted to be an astronomer."[10] But within a few years, writing had lured him back.

He assigns some of the credit for his interest in writing to his father, whom he has described as a born storyteller. At bedtime, John Henderson could usually be persuaded to tell a bedtime story, which he would often invent or adapt while drawing comic illustrations to go with them. From his father's good sense of humor and large collection of jokes, Michael learned how to entertain an audience.

John Henderson had strong opinions about writing, which he imparted to his children. All of them were required to take typing lessons at the age of ten. "My father was a journalist," Michael

Crichton works at his computer. He had wanted to be a writer since childhood.

Crichton explains, "and he believed nobody should write by hand."[11] As a result of those early lessons, Michael learned excellent typing skills, which have helped him throughout his career. Furthermore, John Henderson carried his passion for journalism to the dinner table, where the written word was a frequent topic of conversation. He was a stickler for style and the correct use of language. "My father insisted on clarity and brevity, and he could be a harsh critic,"[12] Michael remembers. As a result, Michael learned to pay close attention to the proper form of writing.

A Difficult Adolescence

Unfortunately, the oldest Crichton child often found himself the brunt of that harsh criticism. In his autobiography, *Travels*, Crichton admits, "My father and I had not had an easy time together. We had never been the classic boy and his dad. And it hadn't gotten any better as we got older."[13] John Henderson had a nasty streak that permanently embittered Michael toward him. In *Travels*, Michael alludes to some physical and mental abuse inflicted by his father. Michael also resented the fact that he could not seem to please his parents. In his mind, they never complimented him, and they belittled his accomplishments. If he came home with a good grade on a paper, they reminded him that it was not perfect and that he needed to work harder.

Nor did Crichton find much comfort among his peer group at school. At an early age he sensed that he was somehow different from other kids, a fact that was reinforced when he hit a runaway growth spurt in adolescence. Gaining a foot of height in a single year, Crichton towered above teachers as well as classmates. His already thin body stretched to the point where he became something of an oddity. As a thirteen-year-old, Crichton stood 6 feet, 7 inches and weighed only 125 pounds; he eventually topped out at 6 feet, 9 inches. Classmates teased and bullied him unmercifully because of his physique.

Crichton also had a sense of being different in personality and interests. Although he enjoyed playing basketball, a sport for which his height served him well, most of his other interests were not as socially popular. "I was a geek," he admits. "I liked to go to the planetarium and to science shows and things like that."[14]

Crichton found refuge in the world of books and pop culture. He especially loved reading the adventure books of Robert Louis Stevenson, a wide variety of science fiction, and mysteries by authors such as Edgar Allan Poe and Sir Arthur Conan Doyle. In a recent online chat with fans, he explained, "I admired Arthur Conan Doyle for the way he made a fictional character, [Sherlock Holmes] seem to be so real that people wanted to find 221 B Baker Street, Holmes' address." [15]

Crichton also became fascinated by motion pictures, especially the innovative classics of director Alfred Hitchcock, who specialized in creating tense, riveting thrillers. "My first hero was Alfred Hitchcock," Crichton has acknowledged. "I knew who he was long before I knew who Charles Dickens was." [16] As he focused on the worlds of science fiction, mystery literature and motion picture thrillers, he became familiar with techniques used to captivate readers and audiences.

Alfred Hitchcock (seated) listens to his daughter Patricia (right) rehearse her lines for a scene in Strangers on a Train. *Michael Crichton considers Hitchcock his first hero.*

A Surprising Breakthrough

For most of his childhood, writing seemed like a far-off and even impossible dream. This changed due to a spontaneous opportunity during one of the Crichtons' summer vacations. The Crichtons believed in exposing their children to different experiences and cultures through travel. By the time he graduated from high school, Michael had visited forty-eight of the fifty United States, Canada, Mexico, and five countries in Europe. One of those expeditions, when Michael was thirteen, brought the Crichtons to Sunset Crater Monument in Arizona. Crichton tells the story in *Travels*:

> I found this place fascinating, but there was nobody else around that day, and I suspected most tourists bypassed it, not realizing how interesting it really was.

Sunset Crater Monument (pictured) in Arizona inspired Crichton to write a travel article about it when he was thirteen years old.

"Why don't you write about it?" my mother said.

"For what?"

"*The New York Times* publishes travel articles from different people." My mother was a great clipper of articles.

"*The New York Times,*" I said. "I'm just a kid."

"Nobody needs to know that."

I looked at my father.

"Get all the published information they have at the ranger stations," he said, "and interview the ranger."

So my family waited in the hot sun while I interviewed the ranger, trying to think of things to ask him. But I was emboldened by the fact that my parents seemed to think I could do this, even though I was only thirteen.[17]

To Michael's surprise and delight, the *New York Times* accepted the article and paid him $60 for its publication. Michael thought he had performed a great feat by writing so well that a professional editor thought he was an adult. Years later he discovered that the *Times*'s travel editor, Paul Friedlander, lived in their neighborhood and that his daughter was in Michael's class at school. Upon reflection, Crichton came to believe that Friedlander knew full well that a teen had written the article, and that he thought it would be an interesting twist to publish a travel piece from a youngster. But at the time, the experience gave Crichton confidence that he already had enough talent to make his mark in the adult world of writing.

From that point on, he began pursuing a writing career in earnest; while in high school he landed a job as a sports reporter for the local newspaper. Although the job paid only ten dollars a week for taking photographs and writing the stories, Crichton enjoyed the work and looked on it as a stepping-stone to a fascinating career. However, at the same time, a nagging voice in the back of his mind told him that his goals were unrealistic. "I wanted to [write] professionally by the time I was in high school," he recalls. "But I didn't think it was possible."[18]

In his rare on-line chats with the public, Crichton frequently credits his public school education with providing a sound foundation for *future paragraph*

Doyle and Crichton

As a boy, one of Crichton's favorite authors was Sir Arthur Conan Doyle. Doyle's early career choices were strikingly similar to those made by Crichton many decades later. Like Crichton, Doyle began his career as a medical doctor, even though he was less than enthusiastic about the field. Also like Crichton, Doyle supported his medical training by writing books; he quickly tired of the medical profession and enjoyed a distinguished career as an author.

The following quote by Doyle, from *Conan Doyle* by Julian Symons, could almost as easily have been written by Crichton many decades later.

> Let me once get my footing in a good hospital and my game is clear. Observe cases minutely, improve in my profession, write to the [medical journal] *Lancet*, supplement my income by literature and then, when my chance comes, be prompt and decisive in stepping into an honorary surgeonship.

his future career. "I was lucky in my schooling, and in my teachers," he has said. "I had a great high school and great teachers." [19] Michael responded well to his teachers' guidance and was ranked as one of the top students in his class. Upon graduation, he was accepted into prestigious Harvard University in Boston, Massachusetts. He set off for the school in 1960 with the intention of majoring in English and learning more about whether it might be possible for him to become a writer.

Plot Twist

But as with the plots of the novels he was later to write, his plans took a sharp and unexpected turn. When Crichton began submitting papers to his English professors, he found their responses far different than that of the *New York Times*. Citing a flawed writing style, his teachers severely criticized his work. Crichton's best efforts earned him no better than a C on his papers. The confidence that for years had fueled his writing ambitions began to evaporate.

Smarting from the comments and searching for answers to his sudden apparent loss of writing skill, Crichton began to wonder if the problem had to do with the way his teachers were relating to him. He devised a dangerous experiment in one of his classes. Upon being given a writing assignment, he remembered coming across an essay that George Orwell had once written on the very same topic. *Orwell* was the pen name of British writer Eric Blair, who is widely regarded as one of the most masterful writers of the twentieth century.

Crichton located a copy of Orwell's essay, retyped it, and handed it in under his own name. Had the teacher been aware of Orwell's essay, Crichton would have been kicked out of school in disgrace for plagiarism. But Crichton felt it was worth the risk to test whether his professor's criticisms were valid. His secret was never found out, and sure enough, the great Orwell's essay managed to earn no better than a B-.

If even Orwell could not satisfy the instructor, Crichton had to question whether the writing courses offered at the school were

Author George Orwell (pictured) wrote an essay that Crichton plagiarized in college.

worthwhile. Under the circumstances, he decided there was no point in butting heads with the English department throughout his college career, and he abandoned his ambition to become a writer.

Despite his experience with the English department, Crichton found the learning atmosphere at Harvard stimulating. "I was very fortunate," he recalls. "In college . . . all my introductory teachers were full professors, individuals of charisma and eminence, imbued with a passion for their field."[20] In such an environment a person like Crichton, who had wide-ranging interests, could easily find another career choice.

Chapter 2

Searching for a Career

ALTHOUGH CRICHTON NEVER had any trouble finding fascinating career possibilities, he experienced a great deal of turmoil trying to turn these possibilities into a solid, established career. In a way, his curious mind proved to be a stumbling block. No matter what area of study he entered, he kept finding himself drawn into some other subject area.

The subject Crichton found most intriguing after abandoning writing was anthropology—the study of the human species and its development—and he set his sights on majoring in that field. However, he was not altogether certain he wanted to go on to graduate studies in that field or what he would do as far as an anthropology career. His lifelong interest in science was growing stronger, and so he decided to study a premedicine curriculum in case anthropology proved a dead end.

He was not prepared for the fiercely competitive nature of premed courses. According to Crichton, if a student was confused about any point in the lectures, the worst thing to do was ask another student for help. Often, other students would give the wrong answer just to gain a competitive edge as they fought to qualify for the few openings in medical school. Crichton's innate clumsiness added to his discomfort in this learning environment. He remembers one of his chemistry courses: "I had the dubious distinction of starting more lab fires than anyone else, including a spectacular ether fire that set the ceiling aflame and left large scorch marks." [21]

Despite frequent doubts that he was doing the right thing, Crichton stuck with the program. At the same time, he satisfied his interest in writing by working for the *Harvard Crimson,* the school newspaper, primarily as a book- and movie-review editor, and by writing sports stories for the *Alumni Bulletin.*

Crichton found that having interest and expertise in several areas provided him with an unusual number of opportunities. On the other hand, it also confronted him with many difficult career decisions. Just when he gained acceptance to medical school, he received an offer to lecture and conduct research on anthropology for a year at Cambridge University in England. Crichton decided the opportunity was too good to pass up, so he delayed his entrance to medical school. During that year abroad, he traveled extensively in Europe and North Africa. He also renewed his interest in reading literary thrillers, finding a spy novel known as *The Ipcress File* particularly fascinating.

Medical School Struggles

Crichton returned to Harvard in 1965, intending to settle down and pursue his medical studies. That same year he married Joan

While at Harvard University (pictured), Crichton changed his major from English, eventually graduating with a degree in anthropology.

Randam, whom he had known since high school. The two rented an apartment in Boston, where Joan pursued her graduate degree in child psychology while Michael studied medicine.

Crichton ran into some immediate problems at Harvard Medical School. For one thing, he had always been squeamish when it came to medical matters. As a child he had hated getting shots and sometimes passed out when he had blood drawn. Now he was frequently required to draw blood from patients, a task that he could manage only with great difficulty. And, on the very first day of class, he was introduced to his cadaver, a human corpse that he was to dissect. Crichton did not want to even touch it. He had hoped that he would be able to overcome some of these attitudes, but after several months he decided he could not take it anymore. His adviser, however, talked him out of quitting medical school, assuring him that the first year was hard on all students but that if he stuck with it, things would improve. Crichton gritted his teeth and kept going.

Meanwhile, there was the question of finances. Now that Crichton was married, he could expect no further funding from his father, who was paying the college tuition bills of his three other children. Since both Crichton and his wife were full-time students, neither was able to earn much money. Crichton turned to writing as a possible source of income.

A Welcome Source of Income

During the 1960s the James Bond novels of Ian Fleming enjoyed wide popularity; Crichton, too, read many of them. As his studies allowed him limited spare time, he decided that Bond-type novels offered the best chance of making considerable money in a relatively short amount of time. Crichton began writing such a novel in 1965, a book that he called *Odds On.* Most beginning authors of fiction have a great deal of trouble getting an editor to read their manuscripts. Fortunately, Crichton had a contact in the publishing world; his father-in-law knew someone who worked at Doubleday, one of the largest book publishers in the country. Although this editor rejected Crichton's book, he put him in touch with a paperback publisher, Signet, who liked his manuscript and bought it.

Writing novels was Crichton's major source of income while he was in medical school.

Odds On was published in 1966 under the pseudonym John Lange. Although the book drew no attention from reviewers, it made enough money that Crichton set out to work on a second similar book. The publication of *Scratch One* in 1967 encouraged him to continue to write paperback thrillers throughout his medical school years. He crammed writing time into weekends and vacations and learned to crank out material at a fast rate. At one time, Crichton estimates, under the strain of tight deadlines with little available time, he was writing ten thousand words a day. In fact, he finished one of his books in just nine days. The first John Lange books were not quality literary works by any means, but Crichton did not particularly care. At this time in his life, all he was interested in was paying bills.

More Doubts

Meanwhile, his medical school experience was not improving; if anything, he found the second year worse than the first. He was especially disappointed in the lectures. Having spent a year lecturing at Cambridge, he knew the preparation necessary to do a good job, and it seemed to him the professors were not taking their jobs seriously. In addition, the classwork and laboratory work were tedious. Again, his adviser told him to be patient. The third year of medical school was when students got out of the classroom and began seeing real patients, and his adviser was certain that Crichton would find that aspect of the field fascinating.

So Crichton plodded on despite his doubts. He did find the interaction with patients during his third year to be more compelling than book work, and he made plans to narrow the focus of his studies to a specialty field. But again, Crichton's attempts to settle into a specific career unraveled almost immediately. His first choice of a specialty area was surgery. However, instead of taking pride in perfecting his surgical techniques, he soon found himself bored with performing the same types of operations over and over. Convinced he could not be a surgeon, he opted for psychology. But the more he met with patients, the more he found that so many of them had problems that he could not help. Crichton began to wonder if psychologists were of any use at all.

At about that time, Crichton noticed that the writing he was doing to support himself was having a curious effect on him. As he states, "Slowly, almost imperceptible, the writing became more interesting to me than the medicine."[22] This produced a terrible dilemma for Crichton. He had worked so hard to get into medical school and to complete much of the coursework. He was capable of some stellar research work, particularly in endocrinology, which would eventually be published in the prestigious *New England Journal of Medicine* and the *Proceedings of the Peabody Museum.* Yet he was finding himself returning to his old dream of a writing career.

Who Was That Mystery Writer?

Prior to this time, the worlds of writing and medicine had been separate in Crichton's mind. That changed when, during his medical rounds, Crichton found himself drawn into what would become one of the most controversial issues in U.S. society—abortion. At that time, abortion was illegal in the United States, which meant that a woman who wanted one had to turn to shady practitioners, whose ineptness often killed or permanently injured their patients. "I saw a lot of the effects of illegal abortions," remembers Crichton. "It was pretty awful. Especially in Boston, nobody would talk about it, but of course I would."[23]

Crichton found the subject of abortion so compelling that he set aside his paperback thrillers and began writing a more serious fiction book on the subject. Instead of racing through the basic elements of plot and setting, Crichton took the time to craft a delicately balanced treatment of a complex social issue within the framework of a mystery. His book *A Case of Need,* which was published in 1968, probed the moral and medical anguish of doctors in cases involving abortion decisions. Crichton was so intent on informing his readers about the subject that, in addition to the story, he included an appendix of medical terms as well as the case for and against allowing legal abortions.

Crichton used his own medical experiences as the backdrop for the book. He based some of the characters on real people and used settings and situations that demonstrated close familiarity with the Harvard University medical system. To protect himself from possible retaliation by superiors who considered themselves slighted by unflattering remarks, he hid behind another pseudonym, Jeffrey Hudson.

Before long, the book created quite a stir in the Harvard medical establishment. It was obvious to all that whoever had written the book had to be on the inside of the medical community, and there was a lot of talk among Crichton's classmates about the author's identity. Crichton found the situation amusing. He had fun joining in the speculation, secure in the knowledge that his secret was safe.

In contrast to his first thrillers, *A Case of Need* was a critical success. Writing in *Best Seller* magazine, reviewer Fred Rotondoro says, "The author has managed to tell a fine story and at the same time comment deftly on some serious contemporary social problems."[24] Readers on both sides of the abortion issue praised the book's balanced and thoughtful approach. In fact, *A Case of Need*

A Missing Lesson in Medical Training

One of the reasons Crichton grew disillusioned with medical school was the cold, impersonal nature of the instruction. In his autobiography, *Travels,* he describes his devastation at being confronted with a dying patient and being unable to relate to him as a human being.

> Arguably the most important item on any medical curriculum, death was never even mentioned at the Harvard Medical School. . . . There was no consideration of what a dying patient went through, what such a patient might need or want. None of this was ever discussed. We were left to learn about death on our own. . . .
>
> When I think back, I imagine the horrible isolation that young man must have felt, sitting day after day in a room that nobody wanted to enter. . . . Instead of having the strength to stay with him, I merely mumbled platitudes and fled. It was no wonder he finally regarded me with contempt. I wasn't much of a doctor: I was far more worried about myself than about him, but he was the one who was dying.

gained such positive recognition that it threatened to unravel Crichton's secret identity. When it won an Edgar Award from the Mystery Writers of America for Best Mystery of the Year, Crichton realized, to his horror, that he would have to accept the award in person, thus revealing his identity. Fortunately for him, however, the medical school world was not tuned in to the world of mystery writers. The awards event went unnoticed at Harvard, and Crichton continued to study unburdened by any hard feelings from the Harvard medical establishment.

Abandoning the Medical Profession

As he gained more success in writing and experienced more frustration with medicine, Crichton's career dilemma grew worse. He found himself disagreeing with a great deal of medical practice and ethics. He chafed at the detached way he was taught to view patients and their symptoms rather than treating them as unique individuals. More and more, he felt alienated from his classmates who seemed so single-mindedly focused on medicine that they ignored most of the rest of life. He found that his creative nature frequently ran counter to the rigid structure of medical training. "I was a little too imaginative," he later commented. "People came to me with their symptoms, and I would look for a new disease."[25]

Crichton had to admit to himself that he found much of medicine boring and that his lack of enthusiasm for the subject was hurting his effectiveness in developing needed technical skills. Comparing the performance of his driven, dedicated classmates to his own, he decided that "these people were professionals of a very high order, and I was a pottering amateur."[26]

Even worse, his growing interest in fiction writing began seeping into his medical practice at the expense of his patients. "I often listened to my patients thinking, 'How can I use this in a book?'" he remembers. "I understood I was not behaving like a doctor that I would want to consult."[27]

By the summer of his third year, Crichton had just about convinced himself to do the unthinkable—abandon medical school. A few months later, while he was still trying to summon the courage to make the break, an incident occurred that clinched that decision. Crichton developed a frightening numbness in one arm. The original diagnosis was multiple sclerosis, possibly a single isolated attack. Although the condition did not prove serious and soon disappeared, the incident shook Crichton. It reminded him that life was short and unpredictable and should not be taken for granted. At that point he decided to stand on his own, face the critics, and do what he wanted, which was to quit medical school and become a writer. But having come within half a year of earning his medical degree, Crichton decided to complete the program before bowing out of medicine.

When he announced his intentions to his family, friends, and fellow students, they were dumbfounded that he would give up such a respected career after doing all of the work necessary to gain it. He recalls, "They were horrified. . . . It was very much like, from their point of view, deciding to not be a Supreme Court Justice anymore, and to become a bail bondsman instead."[28]

Crichton, however, resisted societal pressure and said goodbye to his medical career. Looking back, he has never had any doubt that it was the right decision. "I left medicine as a service to my patients," he told one audience. "I really was a terrible doctor."[29] At the same time, he harbors no regrets about the time and effort he put into medical school. He considered it excellent training for his future career. "Early on it gave me something to write about," he has said, "an area of expertise that I could draw on, a fund of experience and a sense of pace." [30]

Crichton's plan was to move out to California after graduation, where motion picture studios had noticed his work and were in the process of considering *A Case of Need* for movie production. To his

Crichton completed medical school in 1969, but decided not to pursue a career as a doctor.

surprise and relief, the wisdom of his decision to move into the writing world became apparent even before he had finished his last course and had earned his medical degree in 1969. During those last few months of study, Crichton struck gold with an innovative novel, a breakthrough that made him an overnight success and firmly set him on the road to becoming one of the most popular novelists of his time.

Chapter 3

Crichton and the Technothriller

$\mathbf{T}$HE NOVEL THAT was to change Michael Crichton's life began as a title. Long before he had any particular story to go with it, he had devised what he thought was a catchy title for a story: *The Andromeda Strain*. In 1968–1969, the U.S. space program inspired Crichton to finally create the harrowing story to fit that title. At the time, the U.S. government had shown the ability to launch a manned spacecraft to the moon and bring it safely back to Earth. Plans were underway for the historic moon landing of *Apollo 11*, whose mission included bringing back rock samples from the Moon. Microbiologists warned of potential serious problems if any of these space missions encountered microscopic forms of life and brought them back to Earth. Introducing an organism rugged enough to survive in the vacuum of space could be lethal for life-forms on Earth that had no defenses against or resistance to the organism. For that reason, astronauts returning from a space mission were kept in isolation until experts could determine they were free of contamination. The likelihood that a spacecraft would bring back a deadly microbe was small, but precautions needed to be taken nonetheless.

A New Type of Science Fiction

Crichton took this real-life scientific concern and imagined a worst-case scenario. His story tells of a satellite falling to Earth near a small town and the subsequent mysterious deaths of nearly everyone in that town. The rest of the plot revolves around the efforts of four scientists working feverishly at a top-secret Wildfire Project laboratory in the Nevada desert to contain and analyze the deadly microbe, code-named Andromeda, before it causes a widespread catastrophe.

The key to engaging the interest of readers in such a fantastic tale was making it as believable as possible. Crichton accomplished this by making use of the technical and medical knowledge he had acquired in college and medical school to fill the story with accurate scientific details. By building his story brick by brick on proven science and technology, he convinced readers that what he was describing could happen. Furthermore, Crichton displayed such a firm grasp of complex facts and concepts that the average person could not tell when he was describing something real and when he was using his imagination. The book was peppered with computer-generated diagrams and seemingly official warnings. In the book's acknowledgements, Crichton thanked those who helped him in the investigation of the Wildfire Project, making it appear as if the fictitious activity was part of a real government facility. The uncertainty over what was real and what was not made the imagined parts of his story even more terrifying.

The Andromeda Strain was classified as science fiction, but Crichton's book differed from standard science fiction in several ways. First, science fiction at that time generally dealt in speculation about the future. Writers often imagined new technologies and how they would someday impact human life. Crichton's book deals more with the science of the present than with the future. His characters employ the cutting edge technology of science as it existed in such areas as microbiology, computers, and isolation and sterilization procedures to deal with a fictitious but plausible problem, and he describes that science in painstaking detail.

At the same time, Crichton increases the intensity of the story beyond the usual by telling an extremely fast-paced story loaded with dire perils and frantic situations. Furthermore, Crichton's book centers on a timely moral question: What should humankind do to prevent science and technology from creating this horrifying situation?

Critical Reaction

While awaiting the public's reaction to *The Andromeda Strain* in 1969, Crichton was hesitant to make a clean break from the world of academics to the uncharted life of a freelance writer. He allowed

Crichton (second from right) poses with cast members of The Andromeda Strain.

himself a little more time to launch his writing career by accepting an offer for a one-year postdoctoral fellowship to work and study at the Salk Institute for Biological Studies in La Jolla, California.

The success of the book, however, eliminated any lingering doubts Crichton might have had about his future as a writer. The critics generally applauded his innovative work of fiction. *Current Biography* praises the fast-paced story that grips the reader from the beginning and cites the "terrifying air of authority" that comes from the "mass of convincing scientific and technical detail."[31] Because Crichton had reshaped the science fiction novel into a form that came to be known as the technothriller, critic M.B. Wergen writes

In a tense scene from The Andromeda Strain, *a rescuer in protective gear confronts one of only two survivors in a town infected by an organism from outer space.*

in *Library Journal* that *The Andromeda Strain* "must be considered one of the most important novels of the year." [32]

Not everyone, though, welcomed the creation of the technothriller. Alex Comfort of *Bookworld* was particularly upset by the premise of *The Andromeda Strain,* which he described as exploiting the fears of an unwitting public. "Science fiction has undergone an unwelcome change," writes Comfort in reviewing the book. "It used to minister to our need: now it ministers to our fear." [33]

Other critics noted the lack of character development in the book. The book's characters were so bland and generic, said the critics, that the reader never got to know them and therefore could not develop sympathy for them. Crichton admitted that he was not particularly concerned about character development. "It didn't matter who the people were," [34] he says of *The Andromeda*

Strain; he was more concerned with developing the terrifying plot and its implications. He explained that his background in medicine influenced that decision. "Any sense of narrative pacing on my part comes out of the emergency room," he explains. "We don't get to know anybody well, and it's time to move on."[35] He questioned whether a fast-paced book such as his, by its nature, allowed enough time for the type of character development the critics wanted.

The public found *The Andromeda Strain* fascinating. The *Apollo* moonwalk and sample collection that closely coincided with the publication of the book helped fuel that interest and made it a national best-seller. More than 3 million paperback copies of the book were sold. When Universal Studios in Hollywood almost immediately bought the movie rights to the book, Crichton's boundless curiosity was triggered to explore the possibilities of working in the motion picture process.

His career move broke wide open a growing split between Michael and Joan Crichton. She wanted to settle down and have a family while he was focused on his writing career, particularly in the motion picture industry. Joan stayed behind in La Jolla in 1970 while Michael rented an apartment for himself in Los Angeles. For a while, Joan called him almost every day. She wanted to work things out in their marriage and found a psychiatrist to help Michael work out some of his personal issues. The attempt at reconciliation was unsuccessful, however, and the two were divorced the following year. For Michael, the difficulties of his personal life cast a shadow over the exhilaration of becoming a successful, nationally known writer and dabbling in the glamorous world of movies. Though he was a success, he felt lonely and unhappy much of the time.

A Foray into Nonfiction

Despite the runaway success of *The Andromeda Strain,* Crichton did not immediately follow it up with a similar technothriller. And although his main interest at the time was breaking into Hollywood, he turned instead to nonfiction, mining his wealth of experiences in medical school to shed light on the state of modern health care in the United States. Published in 1970, the book titled *Five Patients:*

The Hospital Explained follows the case studies of five patients whom
Crichton had researched while an intern at Massachusetts General
Hospital in Boston over the course of seven months. Critics noted
that Crichton provided valuable insight and was able to "capture
faithfully the atmosphere of a large urban hospital."[36]

From his experience in writing fast-paced thrillers, Crichton
was able to take a potentially dry subject and make it interesting,
while simultaneously raising some timely questions about scientific and medical ethics in the U.S. hospital system. "Crichton is
not only lucid and encyclopedic," comments R. A. Sokolov
about *Five Cases* in *Newsweek* magazine, "but he also manages to
be entertaining. He makes the most technical of information lit-
erally exciting."[37] Affirming that Crichton had the versatility to
create a book far different from his popular thrillers, *Five Patients*
won the Association of Medical Writers award for excellence.
But although it was critically acclaimed, it was not the kind of
story that would interest the Hollywood film community for
which Crichton was interested in working.

Crichton (left) made a cameo appearance in the movie based on his novel,
The Andromeda Strain.

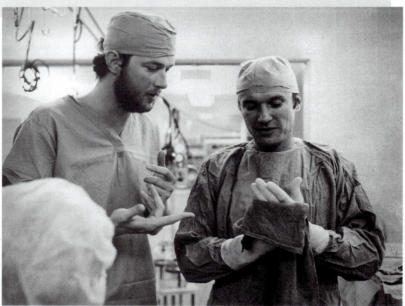

For reasons he has never fully explained, he also continued to write paperback thrillers under the pseudonym John Lange rather than take advantage of the name recognition that came with the success of *The Andromeda Strain*. Of the three titles in the Lange series that he wrote following *The Andromeda Strain*, the most successful was *Binary*, published in 1971. According to Henry Veit, writing in the *Library Journal*, "This is a cliff-hanger all the way, a beautiful jigsaw puzzle, excellently paced to a whiz of an ending." [38]

A Modern-Day Frankenstein

In 1972 Crichton returned to the formula that had made him a media sensation when he published *The Terminal Man*. According to Crichton, "*The Terminal Man* was based on a real patient I saw in the hospital. I can't say anymore about it to protect confidentiality." [39] The plot concerns a man who, as a result of a severe automobile injury, suffers from violent seizures, during which he is extremely dangerous. Doctors at a Los Angeles hospital try to control his illness by implanting a tiny computer-controlled apparatus that produces an electrical shock whenever a seizure begins. The theory is that not only will this procedure short circuit the seizure, preventing its effects, but that the negative reinforcement will cause him to have fewer seizures. Unfortunately, the plan not only fails but also produces an even more dangerous man who escapes the hospital and goes on a rampage. In some ways, it was a variation of the classic Frankenstein story—a physician's honest attempt to restore life instead produces a terrible monster.

Looking to recapture the immediacy and realism that helped make *The Andromeda Strain* popular, Crichton uses two attention-grabbing devices in the introduction. The first is a grim statement advising the reader to take the ethical concerns of the book seriously:

> Readers who find the subject matter of this book shocking or frightening should not delude themselves by also thinking it something quite new. The physical study of the brain, and the technology for modifying behavior through psychosurgery, has been developing for nearly a century. . . . But the public has never really taken it seriously. . . . James V. McConnell of the University of Michigan told

A Master of Technical Information

In the novel *The Terminal Man*, Crichton shows his skill in explaining complex technical information, which becomes an important part of the plot. In this passage from the book, a doctor explains the medical reasons behind the patient's violent behavior.

He went to the blackboard and drew a brain schematically. "Now," he said, "our understanding of the disease process in ADL is that a portion of the brain is damaged, and a scar forms. It's like a scar in other body organs—lots of fibrous tissue, lots of contraction and distortion. And it becomes a focus for abnormal electrical discharges. We see spreading waves moving outward from the focus, like ripples from a rock in a pond."

Ellis drew a point on the brain, then sketched concentric circles.

"These electrical ripples produce a seizure. In some parts of the brain, the discharge focus produces a shaking fit, frothing at the mouth, and so on. In other parts, there are other effects. If the focus is in the temporal lobe, as in Mr. Benson's case, you get acute disinhibitory lesion syndrome—strange thoughts and sometimes violent behavior, preceded by a characteristic aura which is often an odor."

his students some years ago, "Look, we can do these things. We can control behavior. Now, who's going to decide what's to be done? If you don't get busy and tell me how I'm supposed to do it, I'll make up my own mind for you. And then it's too late. [40]

Following this challenge to his readers, Crichton then offers a history of psychosurgical therapy using real dates, people, and events dating back to 1908. As the last entry in this history, he lists the subject of his book, leaving the impression that the incident he is about to describe actually happened.

Crichton has called *The Terminal Man* his least favorite of his books. "I worked on it for nine drafts and never felt I quite got it right," he admits. "I don't to this day know what I would do differently or what I should have done." [41] Critics and audiences, however, did not have the same reaction. In *Best Seller,* Tony Siaulys calls the book, "Crichton's best to date. . . . It all makes for great reading in a number of ways, the most prominent being a topic not so far-fetched that it can be dismissed as something that will never happen. This is a very different piece of science-fiction." [42]

Into the Director's Chair

Crichton had discovered that the technothriller was not just a one-shot success but a sure-fire formula for a literary best-seller. Start with a scientific topic involving cutting-edge research; mix in a situation in which the scientific plans go haywire, putting human beings in danger; and pump out a fast-paced narrative laced with technological descriptions that lend an air of authority to the situation.

Something about Crichton's personality, however, rebelled at following routine, and expected patterns of behavior. Whether it was a case of the grass always looking greener on the other side of the fence or simply a strong need to continually take on new challenges, Crichton kept steering away from success. Just when he had located the key to long-dreamed-of success as a technothriller novelist, he turned his back on it as abruptly as he had abandoned the medical profession. He continued to find himself irresistibly drawn into the motion picture industry.

Up to this point, Crichton's only connection with Hollywood was his ability to sell the movie rights to some of his novels. *The Andromeda Strain* was the first to make it onto the silver screen, coming out as a highly publicized, full-length picture in 1971. The

The character Dr. Mark Hall struggles to escape from the sealed-off laboratory where he and a team of scientists were studying the deadly life-form dubbed Andromeda.

quality of the production was such that, despite having no big-name actors, it received two Academy Award nominations. *A Case of Need,* for which Hollywood had bought the movie rights prior to purchasing *The Andromeda Strain,* finally appeared the following year under the title *The Carey Treatment.* Also in 1972 a book that Crichton had coauthored with his brother Douglas under the joint pseudonym of Michael Douglas made it into film. The story, *Dealing: Or the Berkeley-to-Boston Forty Brick Lost-Bag Blues,* was a lighthearted tale of a Harvard law student who sells marijuana in his spare time.

At first, Crichton experienced the pride of seeing his works reproduced on the glamorous big screen. But that quickly turned to restlessness as he watched other people—screenwriters and directors—change and interpret his creations according to their own ideas. Although he had moved to Los Angeles for the ex-press purpose of transforming his novels into movies, he re-mained an outsider in Hollywood, with only limited input as an adviser. When the experts' adaptations of his films failed to at-tract much of an audience, as in the case of *Dealing* and *The Carey Treatment,* Crichton found it harder and harder to stand by silently. He was determined to gain more control over the movie versions of his works to protect them from the whims of strangers.

He could accomplish this desire in two ways. The most log-ical was to branch out slightly and learn the craft of screenwrit-ing so that he could take on the job of rewriting his own material for the movies. The other was to direct his own movies. Never one to shy away from trying his skill and luck at completely new enterprises, Crichton chose both.

"I'd always wanted to direct movies,"[43] was Crichton's only explanation, noting that the interest went back to the days of his fascination with Alfred Hitchcock films. While visiting the studio sets of his film adaptations and watching the directors at work, Crichton decided he could handle the job. When negotiating a deal with ABC television for the movie rights to *Binary,* Crichton insisted as part of the deal that he be allowed to direct the movie. In the end, ABC agreed and Crichton took the director's chair for the ninety-minute made-for-television movie in 1972. Retitled

Actors Ben Gazzara (left) and William Windom walk with determination in a scene from Pursuit, *a made-for-television movie that Crichton directed.*

Pursuit, the film turned out to be a respectable suspense thriller about a government agent who tries to keep an extremist from devastating a city with stolen nerve gas.

Prior to this, Crichton had always glided from one career interest to another with relative ease, stumbling occasionally but always landing on his feet. The move into Hollywood proved to be a little more unsettling. It would trigger a long period of confusion and several years of writer's block, during which a man who had once fired off ten thousand words a day could not come up with any promising new stories. Year after year would pass with no sign of more technothrillers to come from the man who had perfected the story form.

Chapter 4

Searching for Identity

T HE GLAMOROUS WORLD of Hollywood attracts hordes of fortune seekers, most of whom end up waiting tables or washing dishes in restaurants, hoping for the big break that never comes. Although the success of Crichton's novels opened many doors for him in the movie studios, he, too, experienced the frustrations of trying to establish himself in an unorthodox business. In the process, he began to question who he was and what he wanted out of life.

Finding His Footing

After spending much of his young adult life in the logical, rigidly ordered intellectual world of higher education, Crichton found the atmosphere in Hollywood unsettling. He thought the industry's style of communication was particularly bizarre. It seemed to him that no one listened to him unless he screamed and threw tantrums that would have embarrassed anyone back at medical school. In one case, he repeatedly told a director that a certain actor was wrong for the part yet the director kept the actor on the project. Finally losing patience, Crichton blew up at the director, who then wondered aloud why Crichton had not said anything earlier.

Crichton also realized that he could not trust the people with whom he was dealing. As he writes in *Travels*, "Many things about movies perplexed me. For example, all the people in the movie business lied. They lied all the time. They said they liked your screenplay when they didn't; they said they were going to hire you when they had no intention of hiring you."[44]

Furthermore, the craft of screenwriting is vastly different from writing novels. A screenwriter is limited by time and by the camera in a way that authors can scarcely imagine. Crichton found that a two-hour-long motion picture has no room for the fascinating but rambling asides and explanations of technology that he loved to include in his books. Nor was there time for complicated, drawn-out plot twists. He had to learn through experience that every scene in a movie has to advance the plot and has to be considered in terms of what a camera can record. A character's thoughts, for example, can take up pages of a novel but cannot always show up in film.

It was not until 1973 that Crichton mastered the craft enough to produce his first screenplay for a major motion picture, a spy drama entitled *Extreme Close-Up,* and the effort was not well received. After gaining instant success with his other ventures, Crichton received a cold dose of Hollywood reality in reviews such as the one by film critic Leonard Maltin, whose capsule analysis of the film was, "Ludicrous drama about snoopers and snooping equipment has topicality going for it but that's about all."[45]

Crichton found writing his first screenplay, for a film titled Extreme Close-Up, *challenging.*

Westworld Success

At about the same time, after excruciating negotiations with MGM studios that seemed to be going nowhere, Crichton finally landed a chance to direct a full-length feature film. He had written a screenplay entitled *Westworld* about a virtual-reality park where the super rich could be served by robots in a variety of settings, including the Wild West. In typical Crichton fashion, things go horribly wrong when the technology fails; one of the gun-fighting androids ignores its programmed behavior and runs amok.

In order to land the job of director, however, Crichton had to agree to MGM's demands that he complete the film on an extremely tight schedule and on a low budget. A number of industry experts did not believe it could be done, especially considering the fact that *Westworld* was a futuristic story that required some advanced special effects. Nonetheless, working under intense pressure, Crichton shot the movie quickly and efficiently and came up with a finished product ready for distribution in just six months. Taking advantage of the cutting-edge technology that had long fascinated him, he became the first director to employ computer-generated special effects in a movie.

Given Crichton's limited training and experience in directing, not to mention the restrictions under which he was working, *Westworld* was a surprisingly effective work. Although it did not attract mass audiences in the way that *The Andromeda Strain* and *The Terminal Man* books had, Crichton's realistic portrayal of technology gone haywire influenced other science fiction productions over the years. At the end of the 1970s network television even introduced a new, short-lived science fiction series called *Beyond Westworld*.

A Search for Answers

During the summer of 1973 the initial reaction of critics and audiences indicated that *Westworld* would be a success. Crichton had now achieved an impressive series of successes in a wide range of occupations. He had excelled at anthropology, completed medical school, written best-selling technothrillers and well-reviewed nonfiction, and had now triumphed as a film director and screenwriter. But instead of feeling content at this stage of his life, Crichton fell

Yul Brynner rides a horse in a scene from Westworld. *The movie marked Crichton's feature-film directorial debut.*

into a serious depression. He worried that he had already run out of new challenges and had run himself into an intellectual dead end. He wondered how he would be able to stay alive and focused in the long years of life that still lay before him.

Searching for answers to his dilemma, he sought refuge in the familiar world of books. Impulsively buying anything that might jolt him out of his depression, Crichton would go into a bookstore and purchase five hundred dollars' worth of books at a time. But he was so anxiety ridden that he lost some of his natural curiosity about the world. For a time he could find no subject that interested him. Crichton realized that in his quest for success in publishing and movies, he had cut himself off from the true experiences and pleasures of life. He states, "In my everyday life, I often felt a stifling awareness of the purpose behind everything I did. Every book I read, every movie I saw, every lunch and dinner seemed to have a reason behind it. From time to time, I felt the urge to do something for no reason at all."[46]

Crichton eventually realized that, to find his bearings in life, he needed to follow those urges and to step out of his professional world. He remembered that travel abroad had always relaxed and energized him, and he resolved to travel frequently to exotic places. When Crichton would take off for a few weeks in Malaysia or New Guinea, or go on safari in the African savanna, or climb Africa's tallest peak, Mount Kilimanjaro, friends and associates assumed he was off researching another project. In fact, Crichton took the trips strictly for recreation.

Crichton also began stepping out of his role as the observant, calculating, intellectual scientist to pay more attention to his spiritual side. He began keeping a diary, and he found himself exploring the distinctly unscientific phenomena in the world, such as psychic powers. Over the next decade, this search led him into a wide range of unusual experiences, including detecting auras, spoon bending, and New Age channeling. Crichton came to believe that a range of reality existed beyond that which was explained by scientific study.

Historian

While he was busy pulling out of his depression and trying to come to grips with a new life philosophy, Crichton took up his pen again. But he had no intention of returning to the technothrillers that had made him famous. In his vast store of reading materials, he had finally come up with a subject that fascinated him—one that had nothing to do with science and technology. This was a historically documented robbery of a payroll shipment of gold bullion on its way to the British army fighting during the Crimean War in 1855. The caper was especially intriguing because the thief was an eccentric, well-to-do man from England's upper-class society, who gave no reason for committing the crime other than that he wanted the money.

Crichton researched and wrote a book about the incident, using his active imagination to fill in the details about the heist and the rogues who planned and carried it out. But even though the historical subject was a far cry from Crichton's usual turf, *The Great Train Robbery* carries unmistakable traits of a Crichton book. The story, which was published in 1975, is a fast-paced thriller filled with little-known facts and descriptions. Crichton's plot wanders off on mini-essays about nineteenth-century burial customs, slang, train construction, attitudes toward crime, and dozens of other topics.

But the shift from science to history brought out a less appealing aspect of Crichton's style. In reporting his wealth of information to the reader, Crichton tended to report his conclusions on various issues, such as the root causes of crime, as if they were facts. "I've never read so didactic [obviously intended to instruct] a crime story, or one that so studiously set out to be entertaining,"[47] wrote critic Peter S. Prescott of *Newsweek*. Overall, however, Crichton did succeed in his attempt to entertain as well as teach. Critics and audiences generally found his tale to be, as Prescott described it, "charming, and diverting."[48]

Crichton followed this historical novel with another, even more unusual literary effort with his book entitled *Eaters of the Dead*, published in 1976. The idea for the book emerged in 1974 when a friend of Crichton's included the epic medieval poem *Beowulf* among his list of supposedly classic literary works that no one read willingly

In 1978 Sean Connery (left) and Lesley-Anne Down starred in The Great Train Robbery, *a film based on Crichton's book about an 1855 gold robbery.*

anymore because they were so boring. Crichton disagreed. He believed that *Beowulf* was a gripping, dramatic story, and he offered to prove it by writing a modern version of the story.

In wrestling with how to approach the project, Crichton came up with the idea of using an eyewitness account of the events that *Beowulf* describes. In college Crichton had read portions of a manuscript by a tenth-century Arab named Ibn Fadlan who had traveled north from the Middle East and had written one of the first-known accounts of the Vikings of northern Europe, about whom the Beowulf stories originated. Crichton decided to tell the story of Beowulf through the eyes of the visiting Ibn Fadlan.

To give the story the appearance of reality, he included a substantial number of scholarly footnotes, as if the book were based on real ancient manuscripts. Although Crichton had used similar techniques successfully in other books, the trick was only partially successful this time. For although some critics found the book fascinating, many others thought he had taken the technique too far. Among them was Jack Sullivan, who wrote at the time in the *New York Times Book Review,* "As if to compensate for his undernourished style, Crichton . . . inflates his new narrative with a densely footnoted apparatus of anthropological and literary scholarship. . . . After awhile, this becomes . . . a puzzle that the reader wearies of piecing together."[49] The technique even confused Crichton, who, years later, admitted that he could not remember which footnotes were real and which were based on made-up sources.

Fabricated Footnotes

Scholarly footnotes appear throughout the novel *Eaters of the Dead* to give the appearance that it is a historically documented story. For example, after describing the sighting of a great sea monster, Crichton adds the following footnote.

This account of what is obviously a sighting of whales is disputed by many scholars. It appears in the manuscript of Razi as it is here, but in Sjogren's translation it is much briefer, and in it the Northmen are shown as playing an elaborate joke upon the Arab. The Northmen knew about whales and distinguished them from sea monsters, according to Sjogren. Other scholars, including Hassas, doubt that Ibn Fadlan could be unaware of the existence of whales, as he appears to be here.

Crichton (left) directs Sean Connery (right) before filming a scene for The Great Train Robbery.

Crichton also discovered that, in his search for a dramatic title, he had perhaps gone too far. Many people assumed from the title that the subject of the book was too gory and graphic for them and declined to read it. As a result, when the film version finally came out more than two decades later, he changed the title to *The Thirteenth Warrior.*

Crichton's Peak as a Director

By the mid-1970s other authors with backgrounds in science and medicine had taken up the challenge of writing technothrillers. Among them was Robin Cook, who had not only completed medical school but was a practicing physician. Cook wrote a bestselling book called *Coma,* in which the heroine uncovers a plot by a doctor to induce comas so that he can sell the body parts of his victims for transplants. Based on his success with *Westworld,* a movie studio asked Crichton to write and direct the movie version of *Coma* in 1977. Crichton agreed, and with the help of a critically acclaimed performance from leading actress Genevieve Bujold, the movie did well both at the box offices and among reviewers.

Meanwhile, discussions about the adaptation of *The Great Train Robbery* were coming to a head. Disappointed with the film version of *The Terminal Man,* which had appeared in 1974, Crichton was more determined than ever to shepherd his own books into movie form. With two straight successes as a screenwriter and director under his belt, Crichton proceeded to take on both roles for *The Great Train Robbery* with confidence in 1978.

Unfortunately, he found that working on location in England with an English film crew was far different from working in Hollywood. Crichton had trouble getting the crew to do what he wanted, and as time went on, he detected a distinct lack of respect. Production began to lag behind schedule, and Crichton began to worry whether he could get the film finished at all. In desperation, he asked the advice of one of the most experienced of the film crew, who said little other than to politely ask if he could see a copy of one of the films he had directed. Crichton put him off for a while but finally arranged to have a copy of *Coma* shipped over. Once the crew viewed the film, the work suddenly went smoothly. It turned out that the crew was not convinced that Crichton knew what he was doing, and only after seeing that he had a quality track record would they take him seriously.

In contrast to his other more suspenseful works, *The Great Train Robbery,* starring famed actor Sean Connery as the thief, proved to be lighthearted fun as well as an accurate portrayal of a historical period. The film earned Crichton further praise as a skilled, stylish director.

Losing It as a Writer

Once again, though, Crichton reacted to success as if it were poison. Just as he began to enjoy the respect of his peers as a director, he discovered that he really did not enjoy directing. He found himself in a familiar quandary: He was not content with his current situation, but he was not sure what he wanted to do instead.

At this point, writing was becoming increasingly difficult for Crichton. He had followed up the disappointing *Eaters of the Dead* with a biography of the modern artist Jasper Johns, published in 1977. Crichton worked on the project strictly because of his own longtime interest in Johns, who was too obscure for the book to gain much recognition.

While struggling to discover some writing inspiration, Crichton continued searching for answers to his personal crisis in marriage, travel, and spirituality. In 1978 he married Kathleen St. Johns, a lawyer. However, that marriage ended in divorce only two years later. Ironically, this time it was Kathleen's desire to pursue her career that contributed to the breakup. Crichton followed that up with an equally short and unsatisfying marriage to another lawyer, Suzanne Childs. The experiences left him wondering if there were some serious defects in his personality or character. After his third divorce, he commented, "You may think you are a swell and adorable person, but how many times do you have to get into a traffic accident before you wonder about your driving skills?"[50]

Crichton's travels and his contemplations of the spiritual world seemed to help him regain a little peace of mind, at least enough for him to return to the technothriller, after avoiding the format for eight years. The result was *Congo,* a book that combines the high-tech world of computer technology and innovative research in animal studies with a terrifying adventure in a hidden diamond mine deep in the heart of the African jungle. Published in 1980, *Congo* was, for Crichton's fans, a welcome return to his most comfortable format. Readers were especially intrigued with the character of Amy, a gorilla trained to speak through sign language. Donald Newlove of the *Saturday Review* gave *Congo* high praise, writing: "Michael Crichton is always a gripping hard-science storyteller and here he overflows with energy. . . . Crichton's climax is colossal—volcanic eruptions, earthquakes, an electrical storm dropping 200 bolts per minute. . . . What entertainment!"[51]

Most importantly for Crichton, the subject matter of the book, particularly the signing ape and the jungle perils, attracted an audience that had never shown a great deal of interest in Crichton. Young adult readers, who had previously been turned off by the highly technical subjects of his books, found this book compelling.

Congo, however, drew its share of critics. Some repeated their disapproval of Crichton's creation of characters, noting that he had given Amy the gorilla more personality than any of his human characters. Crichton also drew fire from those who had previously admired his realistic handling of scientific and technological themes. Linguistic experts fumed that the premise of an ape learning complex

The Gorilla Who Could Talk

Crichton drew both praise and criticism for his depiction of Amy, a gorilla who had mastered sign language, in his book *Congo*. Here is an excerpt of the fascinating, yet unlikely, communication between Amy and humans. One of the scientists asks what Amy is going to do tonight.

She gave him the look she always gave him when she thought a question was obvious. *Amy sleep night.*

"And the other gorillas?"

Gorillas sleep night.

"All the gorillas?"

She disdained no answer.

"Amy," he said, "gorillas come to our camp at night."

Come to this place?

"Yes, this place. Gorillas come at night."

She thought this over. *No.*

Munro said, "What did she say?"

Elliot said, "She said, 'No.' Yes, Amy, they come."

She was silent a moment, and then she signed, *Things come.*

Dylan Walsh and the gorilla named Amy read a book together in a scene from Congo.

sign language was ludicrous, leading one critic to describe *Congo* as an "unabashedly silly story."[52]

With the publication of *Congo*, Crichton ran dry as a writer. At that point, says Crichton, "writing was very difficult for me. I did everything I could think of to do. Nothing seemed to matter."[53]

Bottoming Out in Film

If he was having trouble writing, at least he had directing to fall back on, even if it was not his preferred occupation. In 1981 Crichton directed a movie called *Looker,* for which he also wrote the screenplay. The plot concerns a man who attempts to acquire power by using computerized images of gorgeous models in hypnotic television commercials for both products and political office.

All but the most loyal Crichton fans had to admit that he had missed the mark badly. Film critic Leonard Maltin gave the movie his lowest rating. As Maltin puts it, an "intriguing premise is illogically and boringly handled,"[54] harsh words for one whose specialty is riveting technological thrillers. Pauline Kael fired off an even more devastating comment. She writes in the *New Yorker,* "Michael Crichton directs like a technocrat [being more concerned with structures and rules than with people]. This ties in with a small problem he has with his scripts; he can't write people."[55]

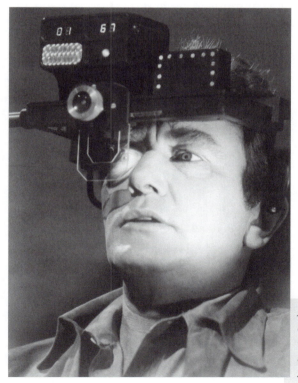

Albert Finney's character tests his reaction to a commercial in a scene from Looker.

Crichton tried to break out of his writing rut by exploring the realm of nonfiction again. Contrary to the writing block that plagued his fiction, the words practically poured out of his word processor as he wrote *Electronic Life: How to Think About Computers,* published in 1983. Written in just four weeks, the book was an attempt to help people intimidated by computers get over their fear and distrust of them.

Crichton tried again to write and direct a quality motion picture in 1984 with the film *Runaway.* This time he did not even write a plausible story line with his tale of a policeman who specializes in tracking down robots who have turned dangerous. Maltin comments that the "special effects are good, but the characters are cold and the story is for the birds."[56] Film critic Janet Maslin of the *New York Times* weighs in with a familiar criticism, that Crichton had a "much better feel for the film's gadgets than for its human players."[57]

Creatively, Crichton had hit bottom. He could not seem to break out of his writing slump, and he appeared to have lost his touch as both a screenwriter and a director. His search for a professional identity had left him spinning his wheels.

Chapter 5

The Blockbuster

CRICHTON CONTINUED TO travel and to explore alternative philosophies in an effort to recapture his creativity. As the 1980s reached the midpoint, Crichton began to fight his way out of his stagnant condition. The author remains unsure to this day as to what extent any of this helped cure his writer's block. All he knows for certain is that it provided him with many interesting experiences and that, sometime in 1985, he was able to refocus on writing. By the end of the decade he would not only be fully engaged in his trademark technothriller format, he would come up with the story that would make him the most famous and successful writer of his generation.

Before he could rediscover his writing talents, however, Crichton ventured into the technical side of film. During the early 1980s he dis-

In the early 1980s, Crichton shifted his efforts from filmmaking to developing computer software.

covered that the movie industry was back in the Stone Age when it came to computers. Thousands of hours were being wasted on administrative and accounting tasks that a computer could handle in minutes.

To fill the void, Crichton created his own software company that developed and sold a computer program that would ease the workload and increase the accuracy of studio accountants. Over the next decade, most studios found the program invaluable. The industry eventually recognized its worth by awarding Crichton an Academy of Motion Pictures Art and Science Technical Award in 1995 "for pioneering computerized motion pictures budgeting and scheduling."[58]

Back to Work

The first fruits of Crichton's resurgence as a novelist was a merging of his most comfortable format, the technothriller, with more traditional science fiction. *Sphere,* published in 1987, tells of the discovery of a huge spaceship a thousand feet below the ocean surface in the South Pacific. The spacecraft is obviously from an advanced civilization yet the evidence shows that it is at least three hundred years old. A team of U.S. scientists is assembled to examine the structure in a dead-sea laboratory. What they find proves to be not only baffling but deadly. As usual, Crichton manages to mix the latest in deep-sea technology and introduce sweeping scientific theories having to do with space travel.

Ron Givens of *Newsweek* was one of many who cheered Crichton's latest effort. "Crichton's writing is cinematic," he wrote at the time, "with powerful visual images and nonstop action. This book should come with hot buttered popcorn."[59]

Settling Down

Although burned three times in marriage, Crichton was ready to try again in 1987. His bride was Anne-Marie Martin, an actress he met on the set of *Runaway.* This relationship proved far more stable than Crichton's previous encounters. For the first time in his life, Crichton was able to settle down and involve himself in a family life. The arrival of his daughter, Taylor, in 1988, provided an even more calming influence. Having a child to care for made him rethink some of his lifestyle habits, including a nineteen-year cigarette habit that he finally discarded.

In 1988 Crichton also made a courageous move for someone who has always been passionate about maintaining his privacy. He finished an autobiography called *Travels,* in which he describes his medical school experiences and his decision to leave, his depression in Hollywood, and the journeys he took to combat it. Included are some very personal revelations about his experiences with his father and with New Age spirituality.

There was something about writing these very personal memoirs that Crichton found freeing. When asked which of his books is the most important to him, he responds, "I liked writing *Travels* best. . . . As I finished each chapter, I had a sense of relief, as if a weight was lifted from my shoulders."[60]

The new, more serene, more focused Crichton who emerged during the late 1980s did not automatically experience success in his projects. He made one more effort at directing, although this time he took on a film for which he did not write the screenplay. Regrettably, the film, a police drama, continued Crichton's losing streak in Hollywood. *Physical Evidence,* released in 1988, won few admirers. Film critics Mick Martin and Marsha Potter place much of the blame on Crichton: "Polished performances by Theresa Russell and Burt Reynolds are wasted in this convoluted police thriller. . . . A thread-bare, erratic plot and haphazard direction by Michael Crichton ruin what could have been a first-rate film."[61] The experience reaffirmed what Crichton had already decided—he needed to get out of directing.

The Seeds of a Megahit

Crichton turned his attention to a new venture, creating a television series that famed director Steven Spielberg was interested in pursuing. While the two met in 1989 to discuss some of the details of the project, Spielberg casually asked Crichton what else he was working on. Normally, Crichton does not like to talk about works in progress;

In 1989 Crichton and Steven Spielberg (pictured) discussed a novel that Crichton had been writing about dinosaurs.

like many writers, he considers it bad luck. But this time he told Spielberg about a novel he was writing that dealt with dinosaurs.

Back in 1982 Crichton had begun reading intensively about dinosaurs. He knew nothing about them when he started, but he quickly had become fascinated by the latest scientific research on the subject. Among the most revolutionary theories were claims by paleontologists such as Jack Horner and Robert Bakker that dinosaurs were not the slow, stupid, overgrown lizards that had commonly been depicted. Recently discovered evidence suggested that they were possibly warm-blooded and the ancestors of birds. Scientists theorized that many dinosaur species were quick on their feet and displayed remarkably developed intelligence and social behavior.

Crichton instinctively knew that dinosaurs would make an excellent subject for a technothriller. They were as huge and as frightening as any creatures of fantasy, and they had actually once trod on the same earth that we inhabit today. They could provide the realistic terror upon which a technothriller depends. The problem was the time gap. Crichton puzzled over the challenge of creating a believable story out of the ridiculous premise of humans coming in contact with a group of animals that had been extinct for millions of years. "My basic strategy was not to make up any more than I needed to,"[62] he recalls. Unless he could come up with a plausible premise out of currently accepted scientific fact, the project would go nowhere.

DNA Cloning

A possible answer to his dilemma came while reading about a 1982 discovery of amber, a form of petrified tree sap, that was found to contain the intact body of a prehistoric insect. The insect had been trapped in the sticky sap, which had hardened into an airtight tomb, preserving it from decay. This opened the door to an ingenious possibility. Suppose a mosquito trapped in amber had just made a meal of dinosaur blood. In that case, the dinosaur blood inside the mosquito would also be preserved. If Crichton could find some way of converting that dinosaur blood into a dinosaur, he would be able to write his story.

Talking to a Cactus

Crichton's spiritual journey led him to some bizarre experiences during the early 1980s. In *Travels* he tells of a psychic healing conference in the California desert during which he was told to find a rock or plant in the desert that related specifically to him. Crichton describes the last of his visits with a cactus:

> The cactus was just sitting there. It wouldn't speak to me. I said I appreciated what it had shown me and I had enjoyed spending time with it, which wasn't exactly true because I had felt frustrated a lot of the time, but I thought it was more or less true. The cactus made no reply.
>
> Then I realized that from its position in the garden the cactus could never see the sun set. The cactus had been years in that position and had been deprived of seeing sunsets. I burst into tears.
>
> The cactus said, "It's been good having you here with me."
>
> Then I *really* cried.

Fortunately, a high-tech possibility for that scenario had presented itself in recent years. The newspapers were full of incredible stories of cloning, a process whereby scientists create a new, living replica of an organism by assembling and growing the DNA from that organism's cells. Scientists were now in the process of accomplishing what just a few years ago had been unthinkable—cloning a mouse.

Even with this new technology, the idea of cloning a dinosaur from preserved blood sounded absurdly far-fetched to Crichton as he groped for ways to build a story around it. Nonetheless, he began writing his new novel, which was, according to Crichton, "a fantastic premise. But since then, technology advanced enough that I began to believe it myself."[63]

In 1984 researchers announced that they had succeeded in extracting DNA from the preserved skin of a quagga, a mammal similar to a zebra that had been extinct for a century. This was quickly followed by a report that scientists had isolated DNA from a forty-thousand-year-old woolly mammoth that had been preserved in a mountain of ice in Siberia. This progression inevitably led to predictions that it was only a matter of time before recovery of dinosaur DNA occurred. Charles Pellegrino, a radical paleobiologist, cleared the way for Crichton in 1985 when he wrote, "We could insert [genetic material] into a cell nucleus, provide a yoke and an eggshell, and hatch our own dinosaurs."[64]

Complaints from experts that old, lifeless DNA was worthless fell to the wayside when scientist Hendrik Poinar found a way to rehydrate DNA so that it regained its ability to produce copies of itself. However, scientists continued to scoff at notions of DNA cloning, observing that, even where DNA was recovered from dead creatures, less than 1 percent of the original DNA survived. Because the DNA was incomplete, many wondered how they could use it to clone an animal.

Again Pellegrino provided a possible answer. Noting that a large percentage of DNA is identical in a wide variety of animals, he suggested simply filling in the missing links in the genetic code with DNA taken from a modern relative. This concept gave Crichton the ingredients he needed for creating a believable way of introducing dinosaurs into the world of humans. And it was this concept that convinced Spielberg, even before the book had been

A menacing dinosaur model stands in an exhibit at the Museum of Natural History in New York City.

written, that he wanted to make the film. Years later he said, "The credibility of the premise—that dinosaurs could come back to life through the cloning of DNA found in prehistoric mosquitoes trapped in amber"[65]—was what guaranteed that this new story would be a megahit.

A Cautionary Tale

Although Crichton was excited about the possibilities that genetic engineering provided for his book, he was disturbed by much of what he read. The field of genetic engineering created profound ethical questions about the wisdom of humans interfering with both the life process and with complex ecological systems. Yet research in this area was advancing rapidly, without much discussion or regulation.

The situation was ripe for shaping the book into one of Crichton's favorite messages: the cautionary tale. In this case, he would warn readers about the dangers of the rash commercializing of biotechnology. He later explained, "Biotechnology and engineering are very powerful. My story suggests that scientists' control of nature is elusive. And just as war is too important to leave to the generals, science is too important to leave to scientists. Everyone needs to be attentive."[66] According to Crichton, that attentiveness needed to start immediately, before genetic engineers created problems that could not be undone. He comments, "Our species has done a lot of things that were hasty or fall into the look-what-I-can-do category. This impulse science, much like impulse buying, needs to be stopped."[67]

Crichton borrowed from two sources in constructing his plot of a bioengineering meltdown. One was a novel written in 1912 by one of his favorite childhood authors, Sir Arthur Conan Doyle, called *The Lost World*, in which a group of explorers encounter grave danger when they come upon a land in which dinosaurs have somehow survived. The other was his own film, *Westworld*. Crichton used the same theme of a fantastic, high-tech entertainment park that destructs under a chain of untimely disasters. Only this time, instead of an amusement park populated with robots, he created a commercial wildlife park stocked with freshly cloned dinosaurs. The mastermind of the park brings in some dinosaur experts as well as his grandchildren to preview the facility before it opens. Gradually, through greed, bad luck, glitches in technology, and unforeseen consequences of the bio-engineering, the park's elaborate safety measures fail, leaving the humans to fight for their lives against the deadly predators. The collapse of the complex park security systems also gave Crichton a forum for one of his pet digressions into a radical scientific topic, in this case the mathematical chaos theory, which maintains that there is always a certain level of unpredictability in complex systems.

Even though the plot was built on the scientific foundations of genetic engineering and chaos theory, Crichton knew he had to do more to make the story real to his readers. The descriptions had to be so vivid and the plot so compelling that readers could experience the terror that the characters were feeling. "The premise is even more unlikely than ET," Crichton later observed. "But one of the ways I can convince you is to be graphic in a Stephen King way—to show you that these are real creatures that can hurt you." [68]

A Novel Tailored to Film?

Crichton's plot included so many frightening, action-packed sequences involving the terror of dinosaurs that the book seemed tailor-made for a motion picture. Critics derided Crichton's books, claiming they were not true literary efforts but merely thinly disguised screenplays for cranking out hugely profitable, blockbuster movies. Crichton, however, has always insisted that the only audience he has in mind when he writes is himself. He notes, "If I tried to guess what other people would like, I think I'd be lost. As a rule, I generally feel when I'm working that nobody will be interested in what I'm doing because it's too technical, or too obscure. Then the book comes out and people *are* interested." [69]

In this case, though, the appeal of dinosaurs coming to life in a scientifically plausible way was as obvious to Crichton as to everyone in the media business. In explaining what he was thinking as he wrote the book, Crichton has given contradictory statements. Magazine profiles in 1990 reported him as admitting that he knew from page one that his book, which he called *Jurassic Park,* would be a smash hit movie, and that he knew he was writing the most expensive film ever made. In a speech to a group of scientists, he gave the impression that the entire project was done with a film version in mind: "It was written to revive the corny movies of people and

The Danger of Genetic Engineering

In the film version of *Jurassic Park,* eccentric mathematician Ian Malcolm sums up Crichton's objection to uncontrolled genetic engineering during an exchange with Hammond, the man who directed the dinosaur cloning.

> Malcolm: If I may, I'll tell you the problem with the scientific power you're using here: It didn't require any discipline to attain it. You read what others had done and you took the next step. You didn't earn the knowledge for yourselves so you don't take any responsibility for it. You stood on the shoulders of others to accomplish something as fast as you could and before you knew what you had, you patented it and packaged it—slapped it on a plastic lunch box and now you're selling it. You want to sell it.
>
> Hammond: I don't think you're giving us our due credit. Our scientists have done things that nobody has ever done before.
>
> Malcolm: Yeah, but your scientists were so preoccupied with whether or not they could that they didn't stop to think if they should.

dinosaurs together that I had loved in childhood. *King Kong, One Million Years B.C.,* all of that. *Jurassic Park* is meant to stand in a long line of related movies."[70]

Perhaps in response to critics who viewed him as more interested in movie profits than in literary excellence, Crichton later shifted his stance. He claimed that he wrote the book knowing that the technology for making a good movie about dinosaurs was not yet developed. "During the time I was making *Jurassic Park,*" he stated in a CNN online interview in December 1999, "it was really impossible to make as a movie. But I wrote it anyway."[71]

The contradictions may have to do with the long period of time during which *Jurassic Park* evolved from Crichton's research. Certainly in the later stage, with one of Hollywood's most influential film directors, Steven Spielberg, eager to make the movie, Crichton was well aware of the commercial possibilities.

"He Can Make the Reader Swallow Just About Anything"

In *Jurassic Park,* which was published in 1990, Crichton creates the ultimate technothriller, combining entertainment with fascinating questions about the role of science in society. Most critics and readers were awed by the book. Gary Jennings of the *New York Times* writes,

With Jurassic Park,
Crichton achieved
enormous success with
both critics and
readers.

It may sound daunting to say that a reader will encounter re-combinant DNA technology, chaos theory, fractal geometry, nonlinear dynamics and even sonic tomography, but Dr. Crichton is adept at making every one of those ingredients comprehensible, often beguiling, frequently exciting.[72]

Director Frank Marshall marveled at how Crichton could make a dinosaur-come-to-life story so believable. "He grounds his fantasy in such contemporary technical reality that he can make the reader swallow just about anything."[73]

There were a few skeptics who missed the point of the book completely. Crichton recalls,

One of the first readers was a well-known molecular biolo-gist. This friend of mine gave him the book and happened to be there when he finished it. The guy slammed it shut and said, "It can't be done!" This was repeated to me with great amusement. And I'm going "No! The whole point of the book is that it shouldn't be done." [74]

But for the most part, Crichton's warning about the dangers of commercial exploitation of science hit the mark, as Peter S. Prescott shows in his *Newsweek* review: "Michael Crichton warns us that we should be afraid, of unregulated genetic engineering in particular. . . . [The book] moves rapidly and manages to be pleasantly didactic." [75]

Motion Picture Phenomenon

Despite the rave reviews and the brisk sales, the novel itself was not enough to turn Michael Crichton into a cultural superstar. It took Steven Spielberg's film talents to accomplish that. Spielberg was so certain that *Jurassic Park* would be a hit movie that he paid Crichton a reported $1.9 million plus a percentage of the profits for the film rights and an additional $625,000 to write the screenplay adaptation.

When Spielberg began work on the film, he faced the same challenge as Crichton, but in a different way: how to make dinosaurs convincing to viewers. Previous movies involving dinosaurs had not come close to achieving anything that resembled a believable dinosaur. Spielberg's team labored for two years and spent millions of dollars before filming ever began to achieve the desired effects. In the end, revolutionary advances in computer graphics helped them create onscreen dinosaurs that looked as though they had actually come to life. Meanwhile, Crichton worked with David Koepp to adapt the story for the screen.

When *Jurassic Park* was released in June 1993 it created an unprecedented response from the movie public. Research scientists unwittingly added to the hype. Shortly after the film was released California biologists Raul Cano and George Poinar Jr. announced the cloning of DNA from a 40-million-year-old bee. At almost the same time, the American Museum of Natural History in New York cloned DNA from a 15-million-year-old termite trapped in amber. The announcements made the events of *Jurassic Park* seem even more plausible and therefore more frightening.

Some critics were disappointed in the story line, which they felt glossed over or ignored the most fascinating parts of the book. Critic David Thomson calls the film "comically bereft of any character or purpose except that of making marvels and money." [76]

Most critics, however, declared *Jurassic Park* to be jaw-dropping, breath-taking entertainment. Brian Johnson writes in *Maclean's*, "It is such a staggering spectacle that its shortcomings seem almost beside the point." [77] Peter Travers of *Rolling Stone* agrees, declaring,

Joseph Mazzello, Sam Neill, and Ariana Richards (left to right) feed a friendly Brachiosaurus in a scene from Jurassic Park.

"*Jurassic Park* is a grabber for the best of reasons: You won't believe your eyes." [78]

From the beginning, the movie shattered all previous box-office records. It eventually earned more than $900 million worldwide, making it the most successful movie in history (since topped by *Titanic.*) As the author of the story, Crichton instantly became one of the most widely known authors in the world.

Chapter 6

The Media Celebrity

ALTHOUGH THE SUDDEN explosion of fame that Crichton experienced following the release of *Jurassic Park* may seem like a dream come true to most struggling artists, a person who is unprepared for it can be knocked off balance and lose his or her perspective on life. With Crichton's settled family life offering stability, he was in a better position than in previous years to navigate the turbulent waters of fame.

Privacy Issues

The biggest problem with fame was that, despite Crichton's long fascination with the glamorous world of film, he remained an extremely private person. He was uncomfortable in the spotlight and wary of the demands of the media. When asked about all the attention he was attracting, Crichton says, "I chose my life to be behind the camera in all the ways that that implies. You know, I chose my life to be unrecognizable and now I find that I'm not unrecognizable."[79] Crichton had to acknowledge that he was in a business in which publicity was a key ingredient of success. He had to strike a balance between making personal appearances and statements to generate interest in his projects and preserving his private life.

One area of his life that was strictly off-limits to reporters was his home. He tells *Architectural Digest* magazine,

> We live in a show business environment where people's lives are often constructed to be featured on a TV show and everything is available for promotion. This house was off-limits. We didn't entertain much. If the house impressed no one, that was fine with us. We came home to collapse and recuperate.[80]

At the same time, he did not let fear of publicity hounds nudge him into a world of isolation and seclusion. Unlike many stars, he did not necessarily change his habits just because he could afford a more luxurious lifestyle. For example, he believed there was no better way to keep in touch with the movie-going audience than to be one of them. He once commented, "I would never have a screening room. I want to go to the movies. I stand in line like a regular person—I've been doing that for twenty years. It's a valuable policy. Standing in line gives you lots of information."[81]

Grabbed by a Story

The greatest advantage of Crichton's newfound fame was that the very mention of his name was enough to get people interested in his projects. All a publicist had to do was slap "from the author of *Jurassic Park*" on his work and it was sure to attract attention. Publishers even reissued old books, such as *A Case of Need,* that he had published under a pseudonym, this time with Crichton's name on it.

Success has forced Crichton to negotiate a balance between keeping in the public eye and preserving his privacy.

When it came to his next projects, this fame simultaneously pulled him in two directions. On the one hand, his reputation was so strong that he was free to try virtually anything he wanted and publishers would buy it. On the other hand, he came under intense pressure to stick with a formula that worked and write another of his trademark technothrillers.

Crichton had never been interested in routine, however, and he was not about to start now. Free to explore whatever facets of life he found interesting, he simply went wherever his interests took him. As usual, he had no master plan for his career. When describing how he chose a subject for a new book, he explained that his natural curiosity frequently dictated what he would do. "Often I feel grabbed by a story and yanked into the office to start writing,"[82] he says.

The story that grabbed him immediately after *Jurassic Park* was a far cry from his usual subject matter. Crichton became engrossed in the subject of international economics, specifically, the economic competition between the United States and Japan. The more he read, the more he became concerned that the two nations were not playing by the same rules. The United States had an open system whereby the government basically let the marketplace decide whether businesses succeeded or failed and it encouraged free trade between nations. In Japan, Crichton came to believe, government and businesses worked as a team to advance the nation's economic interest over those of its international competitors. In the long run, Crichton believed, this would weaken the United States as a nation. During the early 1990s, these fears were reinforced by a slowdown in the U.S. economy and by news reports that Japanese investors were buying up long-established U.S. businesses and institutions as well as large chunks of real estate.

A Storm of Controversy

Crichton wrote a novel titled *Rising Sun,* published in 1992, that he hoped would awaken complacent Americans to the industrial threat that Japan posed. As usual, he wove his message into an elaborate, fast-moving, suspenseful plot, laced with a flurry of facts that he had accumulated. The plot concerns a young woman who is found murdered on the forty-sixth floor of a Los Angeles building that is the American headquarters of a giant Japanese corporation. During the

Japan-Bashing?

Crichton's assessment of Japanese business practices in *Rising Sun* brought howls of outrage from critics who viewed it as Japan-bashing. Crichton countered that he was just telling the unpleasant truth. The following statement about Japan by the book's hero, John Conner, is a sample of what caused the furor.

> Business is like warfare to them. Gaining ground. Wiping out the competition. Getting control of the market. That's what they've been doing for the last thirty years.
>
> So the Japanese dumped steel, televisions, consumer electronics, computer chips, machine tools—and nobody stopped them. And we lost those industries. Japanese companies and the Japanese government target specific industries, which they take over. Industry after industry, year after year. While we sit around and spout off about free trade. But free trade is meaningless unless there is also fair trade. And the Japanese don't believe in fair trade at all.

course of the investigation, an American detective encounters a web of deceit and secrecy that is part of a larger struggle between Japan and the United States for control of vital technology. Crichton uses his trademark technique of building realism into the story by including apparently factual documentation, this time in the form of an official "confidential" transcript of a video interrogation that supposedly came from the Los Angeles Police Department files.

Crichton pulled no punches in describing the Japanese as formidable and dangerous business competitors. One of his characters accuses the Japanese of being the most racist people on the planet. Anticipating that his book would draw criticism as a gross exaggeration of the situation, he included a lengthy bibliography of scholarly sources upon which he based his conclusions.

Predictably, *Rising Sun* generated a storm of controversy unlike anything Crichton had previously experienced. On the positive side, *Current Biography* hailed it as "without a doubt the most influential and controversial of Crichton's novels to date" and a "realistic, densely plotted murder mystery."[83] The *New York Times* ran a front-page review of *Rising Sun* in its book review section. Critic Robert Nathan urged readers to take Crichton's work seriously. "Despite the book's provocative tone," he writes, "Mr. Crichton is no xenophobe [a person with an unreasonable fear of foreign people], no fool, no ranting bigot."[84]

But Crichton took some heavy hits from other reviewers around the country. According to Karl Taro Greenfield in *Nation* magazine,

> Crichton has brought to the surface an idea that has been lurking for some years in America's collective pop-culture subconscious: The Japanese are evil. . . . If African-Americans or Jewish-Americans were portrayed in a similarly negative caricature, there would be storms of protest. [85]

John Schwartz of *Newsweek* also took Crichton to task, saying that *Rising Sun* was a "classic paranoid thriller, which is not to say that he works hard at proving his case. When he wants to bash, he just has a character express an opinion." [86]

A Big Year at the Movies

The criticism did nothing to dampen sales. In fact, the combination of Crichton's success with *Jurassic Park* and the publicity generated by his new novel made *Rising Sun* a hot product in the film industry. Crichton originally signed on to help write the screenplay for the movie version of the book, for which veteran director Philip Kaufman obtained the rights. Sensitive to the drubbing the book was getting in the press for its aggressive stance against Japan, however, Kaufman began insisting on wholesale changes to the plot and characters that would take away some of its abrasive edge.

Crichton thought the changes were watering down his story to the point where its message was lost, but since he had sold the screen rights, he had no authority on the project. When Kaufman insisted on doing it his way, Crichton refused to have anything more to do with the film. In fact, he did not even want his name listed among its screenwriters.

According to critics such as James M. Welsh, the film was an unsatisfying version of Crichton's work. "Kaufman remade the novel in such a way that its cultural contrast was softened and made 'politically correct,'" [87] writes Welsch. Nonetheless, the film's stars, Sean Connery and Wesley Snipes, delivered widely praised performances and *Rising Sun* did well at the box office when it was released in late 1993. Even though Crichton disowned the film, its success rubbed off on him. He became the first living author to have two recently published books made into hit movies in the same year. His reputation as a gold mine for Hollywood film studios rose yet another notch.

The Battle of the Sexes

Crichton's next book further confounded readers who had been awaiting another of his technothrillers. This time, he wandered into a common literature theme far removed from the world of science —the relationships between the sexes.

As a man who had had three marriages and was on his fourth, Crichton had experienced his share of the joys and frustration of sexual attraction and compatibility. In his book *Travels* he writes about some of his puzzlement over the repeated sources of misunderstanding between men and women, and details his efforts to determine in what ways men and women were alike or different.

During the early 1990s the issue of sexual harassment in the workplace grabbed national attention, highlighted by accusations of improper behavior that surfaced in the widely publicized Supreme Court confirmation hearings of Clarence Thomas. This presented Crichton with a hot topic through which he could explore his musings about the conflict between men and women.

As always, Crichton looked for a fresh angle on the issue to capture his readers' interest. The typical workplace sexual harassment involved males who made unwanted sexual comments or advances to female coworkers. In many cases, it was male executives who were accused of mistreating women who worked for them— women who might be reluctant to say anything for fear of losing their jobs. Crichton found his fresh angle in a story a friend told him about a real-life workplace incident in which the tables were turned: A female executive was accused of harassing a male employee.

Disclosure, published in 1994, used the same premise: an aggressive female executive makes life miserable for a male employee under her supervision who rejects her sexual advances. Crichton displays his technology expertise by using a high-tech computer company as the setting for the incident and by having the main character unravel the company's secrets by uncovering an electronic trail of evidence.

Although Crichton again was plowing into a politically sensitive area, *Disclosure* did not provoke nearly the outrage of *Rising Sun*. Typical of the critics' reaction was that of Michael Coren in the *National Review:*

> Mr. Crichton has done more than question the conventional wisdom about sexual harassment: he has turned that wisdom completely on its head. . . . This is provocative stuff. . . . On one level *Disclosure* is a literary pebble tossed into a political pond, and the ripples just might dampen some of the strident howls and emotional spasms that currently dominate discussion of the issue. On another, it is a refreshingly uncluttered and sinewy entertainment, free of pretension and eminently readable.[88]

As expected with such a controversial topic, there were those who raised objections. Some critics said that Crichton was exploiting a serious political issue just to sell books and make movies. In fact, Crichton was raking in money hand over fist. By 1994 more than 100 million copies of his books were in print. The film rights

Michael Douglas confronts Demi Moore in a scene from Disclosure.

The Author Explains

Crichton often feels compelled to comment on the issues of a particular book, either in the foreword or the afterword. The following is from the afterword of *Disclosure*.

The episode here is based on a true story. Its appearance in a novel is not intended to deny the fact that the great majority of harassment claims are brought by women against men. On the contrary: the advantage of a role-reversal story is that it may enable us to examine aspects concealed by traditional responses and conventional rhetoric. However readers respond to this story, it is important to recognize that the behavior of the two antagonists mirrors each other, like a Rorschach inkblot [psychological test]. The value of a Rorschach test lies in what it tells us about ourselves.

to *Disclosure* sold for an astonishing $3.5 million. It became a major motion picture in 1995, starring Demi Moore and Michael Douglas, followed quickly that year by a film version of *Congo*.

Crichton's supporters argued, however, that the fact that his books made money should not be taken as proof that they were not serious works. They insisted that his interest in all of the issues of his novels was genuine, his research was thorough, his treatment honest, and his conclusions reasonable. The fact that he could sell books while exploring serious topics was a testament to his ability to communicate these serious subjects to the average reader with flair. As for his topics, Crichton insisted that he chose subjects not for their shock value but because he found them fascinating and thought provoking.

The One and Only Sequel

Ever since *Jurassic Park* first hit the shelves, fans begged Crichton to follow it up with another story about genetically engineered dinosaurs. Publishers and motion picture financiers also put pressure on him to produce a sequel. Crichton had become accustomed to this kind of pressure. His closest rival as a technothriller author, Tom Clancy, who specialized in military technology, had shown how profitable this could be. By basing a series of books on the character of Jack Ryan, Clancy had built up a huge and loyal following. Crichton felt pressure to do the same, as he describes: "There is an internal and an external pressure to keep doing the same thing. People liked it. You got rewarded and praised for it. So do it again! The same, only different. So it becomes something you have to fight." [89]

For years, Crichton fought off the urge. He had the type of personality that was always interested in looking forward, not backward, and throughout his career he had carefully avoided falling into any rut or routine that would dampen his enthusiasm. He had never done a sequel to any book, and he never intended to. "I'm a clean look in any given area," he explains, "and I'm a single look." [90]

But after completing *Disclosure,* Crichton eventually yielded to the wishes of his *Jurassic Park* audience, although he was careful to note, "If I hadn't found a story I was interested in, *Jurassic Park* would have remained a nice memory for me." [91]

The story that Crichton developed was the discovery of the existence of an island in Central America that had served as a holding pen for some of the dinosaurs created by the genetic engineering experiments to stock the original Jurassic Park. In the sequel, three groups of people arrive on the island: one to exploit the creatures for commercial gain, another to study the behavior of dinosaurs as they live in the wild as opposed to the artificial park of book one, and the other to stop the nonsense and rescue those who do not realize the terrors into which they have stepped.

Crichton again drew on the work of his favorite boyhood author, Sir Arthur Conan Doyle, in two ways. First and most obvious, he titled the novel *The Lost World,* which was also the title of Doyle's 1912 dinosaur novel. Secondly, he revived his favorite character from *Jurassic Park,* the wise-cracking mathematician Ian Malcolm, who had apparently died at the end of the first book. Crichton noted that he needed Malcolm for the book and that Doyle had established a precedent by killing off Sherlock Holmes in one book and resurrecting him without explanation for later novels.

Since it was a foregone conclusion that *The Lost World* would be eagerly snapped up by the millions of fans of *Jurassic Park,* Crichton was able to command an enormous advance for the book and the publisher cranked out a record 2 million copies in its first printing.

In general, however, neither readers nor critics were as enthralled with the sequel as they had been with *Jurassic Park*. Again, there were complaints that Crichton was merely cashing in on another surefire box office winner. Mark Annichiarico writes in *Library Journal,* "This much anticipated sequel to the megahit Jurassic Park reads more like a movie novelization: so bereft of plot and characterization in deference to action that it is closer in spirit to Steven

Richard Schiff, Julianne Moore, Jeff Goldblum, and Vince Vaughn (left to right) run for their lives in a scene from The Lost World.

Spielberg's movie version than the entertaining and educational novel that preceded it."[92]

Sure enough, Spielberg also turned *The Lost World* into a blockbuster movie. But again, critics and fans felt it fell far short of the original effort in terms of creativity and believability. All in all, Crichton decided that his initial instincts had been sound; he vowed that he would stay away from sequels in the future.

Chapter 7

Looking for New Challenges

Michael Crichton has never stopped seeking new challenges to his creative energy. During the decade of the 1990s, he ignored media investors who advised him to cash in on his *Jurassic Park* fame by producing a series of related novels and movies. Crichton was not interested in creating an industry. As always, he followed his curiosity. Crichton explored new topics as well as new media for presenting his ideas.

Even before *The Lost World* reached the public, he was already ranging far afield from his trademark technothriller novels and screenplays into yet another new area. From the fantastic world of rampaging dinosaurs, he turned to a gripping real-life television drama. In place of the big-budget, blockbuster motion picture, he created a long-running series for television.

ER

The project was called *ER*, and Crichton had invested many years of effort to bring it to the small screen. Ever since his medical school experience in the emergency room of Massachusetts General Hospital in Boston, Crichton had been interested in creating a television series based on the everyday life-and-death challenges of emergency room personnel. It was Crichton's way of paying tribute to the many dedicated doctors, nurses, and technicians that he had encountered during his medical training. He explains his motivation for the project:

> I think that we've had a long period in which doctors are
> denigrated in various ways. And there are places where

doctors continue to perform as well as they can, as skillfully as they can, and really do heroic actions. And I wanted to sort of bring that back into balance—have doctors who are like that.[93]

In 1974 he put together a script for a pilot episode of *ER* and shopped it around to television executives. Nobody was interested. For fifteen years Crichton collected nothing but polite rejections. "It took a long time to get made because nobody wanted to do it," he remembers. "It was seen as too fast-paced, too focused on doctors and not patients, too technical."[94]

In a scene from ER, *medical personnel prepare to treat a trauma patient who has just arrived at the hospital.*

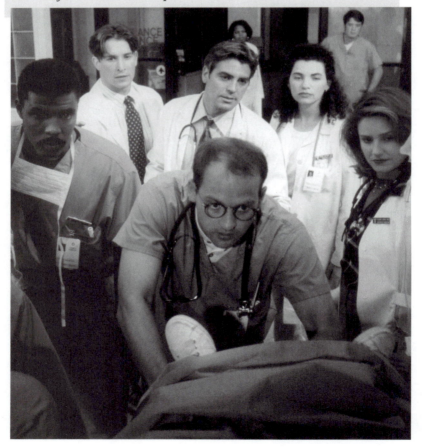

Crichton, however, refused to give up on his dream. Finally, as he tells an online audience, he got a nibble:

> What actually happened was in—I think 1989, Steven Spielberg called me up and said he wanted to do a project about an emergency room, and I said I did too. And we began to work on this thing, and shortly after that he got interested in dinosaurs and I did too. So we deferred this thing.[95]

Finally, however, Crichton's patience was rewarded, as the influential Spielberg eventually helped shepherd the project through network television's red tape. Crichton became heavily involved in the production of the show, including writing the first episode. He was not interested in being tied to a demanding writing schedule, however, and once past the initial episode, he left the writing to others. In 1994, twenty years after Crichton had written the original script, *ER* finally appeared on NBC television. Ironically, it appeared in the same time slot as another network show on a similar topic, *Chicago Hope.*

It was *ER*, however, that captured the interest of television viewers. In 1994–1995 the show posted the highest television ratings ever for a first-year dramatic series and the best ratings for any television drama in the past ten years. The show, which helped make a star of lead actor George Clooney, continued to attract huge audiences through most of the 1990s.

The Reader

Going into the mid-1990s, Crichton was on the most incredible roll of any storyteller in modern history. He had written four runaway best-selling books in rapid succession. All of the books had been made into successful major motion pictures, and one of them had become the most popular motion picture in history. On top of that, he now had created the top-rated show in television. Everyone wondered how he had accomplished this.

For Crichton, the process begins with reading. Crichton is extremely well read, and as the wide range of his book topics proves, there is no predicting what subject matter will appeal to him. However, he seldom settles for light reading; his bibliographies are filled with such daunting titles as *The Fabric of Reality: The Science of*

Parallel Universes and Its Implications and *The End of Laissez-Faire: National Purpose and Global Economy After the Cold War.* "I read mostly non-fiction (95 per cent of the time) and mostly in some particular subject area that I am studying for a new project,"[96] he explains. When he is not reading books, he is often combing through piles of magazines, many of them technical ones.

For years, Crichton used to tell people that he did not do research at all. But he has come to realize that although he does not do research in the usual methodical, documented way, he nonetheless spends a great deal of time collecting information. Rather than filling notebooks with facts, he stuffs them in his mind. Occasionally, he will consult with an expert in a particular field to prove to himself that he understands the most current and advanced concepts.

"I think what happens is that I read in an area for a long time— usually years—and when I finally get around to writing the thing, I'm pretty well-informed. . . . I have been tracking a subject like hot-blooded dinosaurs for years,"[97] he says. When it comes time to write, he seldom refers to notes. "I start with a fairly well-worked-out plan that has [been] percolating for some while, maybe five years."[98] Crichton does not like to paint himself into a corner—that is, to cre-

Violence on the Screen

Although Crichton's books contain a fair amount of graphic violence, he strongly advocated taming down the gore in the movie version of *Jurassic Park,* as he indicates in these two passages. The first passage is from Brian D. Johnson's article "Myths in the Park," printed in *Maclean's* in June 1993; the second is from a November 2, 2000 online interview with John Callaham from www.stomped.com.

> In a book, you are your own film maker and you'll see what you want to see. In a movie you are being shown images that you can't control. If you see intestines pour out, you go, "How did they do it?"

> I think we are entering a period of intense scrutiny of violence and explicitness in all our media. I don't think it's a bad idea. My own opinion is that from an aesthetic point of view, things have gotten out of hand. We now have meretricious [gaudy] crudity and explicitness everywhere. . . . Our society may collectively decide to exert pressure to tone down all the gore and swearing and flesh, just because we find it unpleasant and off-putting. I think that may happen.

ate an impossible situation and then search for some way out. Rather, he tries to research all possible technical problems in advance and devise realistic solutions to them.

A Constant Struggle

"I find research is fun for me," says Crichton. "I enjoy it!"[99] He does not say the same about the actual writing of a novel or a screenplay. He has said that he does not particularly enjoy the work of writing, that he finds it extremely strenuous. Surprisingly, for a person who has written so much, words do not come easy for Crichton. "My own experience of writing is one of constant struggle,"[100] he admits.

Because he finds it such exhausting work, Crichton cannot bring himself to sit down and write on a regular basis. "I'm not an everyday writer, and I never have been," he explains. "I have a continued pattern of intermittent, very intense effort, and that's the way I still do it."[101] As with all writers, Crichton has periods when everything clicks together and the words flow, and other times when he has to wrestle with every sentence.

> Sometimes I have a good plan and I work regularly. At other times . . . I just struggle and revise and rewrite—give up in discouragement for months on end, then drag myself back to it, then get an okay draft, then make a little progress, then give up again . . . then try again.[102]

Long gone are the days when Crichton could crank out ten thousand words a day. He is a more refined writer today, and he now considers twelve hundred to twenty-four hundred words a good day.

As critics frequently point out, Crichton tends to struggle with characters. But he insists that he does not write for the critics. In fact, the only audience he considers is himself. "I think it is every writer's experience that I imagine myself to be all the characters, you know. They're all my children I love them equally. So far."[103]

Crichton has found that setting up a rigid routine helps keep him on track through the difficult stages of writing. For example, when he is writing he eats exactly the same thing for lunch everyday. During the writing of *Congo*, this meant a steady diet of mashed potatoes, gravy, and open-faced turkey sandwiches.

Crichton holds a pocket PC to demonstrate that his novel, Timeline, *is available for immediate download.*

Crichton prefers to work when it is quiet, usually in the early morning or very late at night. The further he gets into a book, the more obsessed he becomes with finishing it. During the writing of the first draft, which generally takes about six to ten weeks, he wakes up around 6:00 A.M. to start work. As he becomes more engrossed in the project, he becomes more restless. He begins waking up earlier and earlier to write. Eventually, when his workday begins at 2:00 A.M., he realizes that he has hit the point of no return: He must work steadily on the book to get it finished before he collapses from exhaustion. For Crichton, the writing process requires an average of about eighteen months per book.

Crichton cannot explain how he transformed himself from a successful writer during the 1960s through 1980s into the most phenomenally successful author of his time during the 1990s. But he gives some of the credit to the settling influence of his family. Although he does enjoy leisure activities such as wilderness hiking, water sports, traveling to exotic places, collecting modern art, and cooking, he appears content with splitting the vast majority of his time with his work and his family. "It seems like in a way, that's all there is," [104] Crichton now says.

A Hollywood Winning Streak Ends

Crichton's track record for success during the mid-1990s was so impressive that book publishers and movie executives all but leaned over his shoulder as he wrote, hoping to snap up whatever the author produced next. The next book off the press was *Airframe,* published in 1996. In it, Crichton grabs the reader with a harrowing and mysterious breakdown of technology. Flying at thirty-five thousand feet, a twin-jet airliner flying from Hong Kong to Denver suffers a violent accident that claims the lives of three passengers and injures fifty-six others. With the future of a billion-dollar corporation at stake, an investigator is sent to piece together what went wrong to prevent a repeat accident from ever occurring. She discovers, however, that some powerful people have a secret they do not want her to uncover.

Critics were generally favorable. Roy Olson of *Booklist* saw the book as a typical, solid Crichton effort. "Loading it with interesting detail on airline construction and aerodynamics, the international trade in commercial aircraft, and air safety, Crichton produces a taut, absorbing suspensor anyway," [105] he writes.

John Lanchester, in the *New Yorker,* was among a number of critics who thought they detected a growing trend in Crichton's books. "It is increasingly apparent that [Crichton] is deep down, a moralist," writes Lanchester. "He now concentrates more and more on much debated issues of the day, which he picks up and turns into novels with a point of view and a moral." [106]

Like all of Crichton's recent novels, *Airframe* became a national best-seller, although skeptics claimed that with Crichton's reputation, he could put his name on a phone book and sell one hundred thousand copies. Unlike his other books, however, *Airframe* was less action oriented and did not easily lend itself to a movie adaptation.

Disappointed motion picture executives passed on the project, breaking Crichton's unprecedented streak of hugely profitable film adaptations.

Time Travel

The unpredictable Crichton then returned to the standard Hollywood success formula by cowriting with his wife, Anne-Marie, the screenplay for the popular special effects–loaded film *Twister* in 1996. But he again broke with convention by following this with a journey into the decidedly low-tech world of medieval history. He did manage to mix in science and technology, though. But, even more surprisingly for someone as stubbornly original as Crichton, he did so by resorting to a theme that had become commonplace in modern science fiction literature—time travel. Furthermore, he went back to a plot device he had tried twice before—using technology and unlimited funds to create a revolutionary theme park. In his book *Timeline,* published in 1999, a billionaire uses time travel to send historians working on an ar-

Bill Paxton and Helen Hunt run for safety in Twister.

chaeological dig back to fourteenth-century France to collect information for a historical theme park.

But Crichton showed that he was not merely going through the motions by recycling well-worn ideas. Although other time-travel writers had glossed over the actual technology of time travel and just asked readers to assume it was a possibility, Crichton insisted on making it real. His time travel technique was described in elaborate detail using the latest findings on the revolutionary physics field of quantum mechanics. He then went on to thoroughly research fourteenth-century France to give the reader a vivid and accurate picture of what his time travelers encountered. Crichton then added spine-tingling suspense by having the travelers land in the middle of a fierce war, based on his historical findings of a war in 1357.

Timeline joined the parade of Crichton books on the best-seller shelves and drew high praise from critics. "As taught by Crichton," writes Daniel Mendelsohn in the *New York Times Book Review,* "the Middle Ages are a lot more interesting than you remember from your 10th-grade history class. . . . With Crichton you get the really cool minutiae." [107]

What Is Next?

Given Crichton's wide-ranging and random selection of topics, it is not surprising that the most common question he hears from devoted fans of his work is, "What's next?" Ever superstitious about speaking of new projects before they are finished, he refuses to reveal what he has planned. He has said that he has no plans to return to directing. In his view, the film industry has stagnated into a period of "remakes and recycled ideas" [108] that stifle creativity.

In view of Crichton's history of sudden career changes, it is doubtful that even he knows what lies ahead. He steadfastly refuses to let himself slide into a rut of repeating his past successes, regardless of how much money he could make by doing so. Crichton is always on the lookout for new challenges, and he has demonstrated the intelligence to quickly grasp the basics of virtually any new technology. In 1999 he branched into yet another new career when he formed a company called Timeline Studios to market video games he has invented. He has proven to be utterly fearless in trying new ventures, an attitude that comes from his acceptance of failure. "I think if you don't fail a certain percent of the time, it means you're playing it too safe. You're obligated to miss sometimes." [109]

Predicting Crichton's future subjects is impossible because Crichton, who once was tormented as a child because he did not blend in with other kids, has come to take pride in being different and unpredictable. He compares himself to a bat: "Feeling conflicted, different, has been a fact of my life. Put a bat among birds and they call it a mammal. Put it among mammals and they call it a bird. . . . I don't seem to fit in anywhere." [110] But, whatever he does, science is certain to wind up somewhere in the mix. It remains Crichton's passion: "Science is the most exciting and sustaining enterprise of discovery in the history of our species. It is the great adventure of our time. We live today in an era of discovery that far outshadows the discoveries of the New World five hundred years ago." [111]

The Crichton Legacy

Crichton's attention to detail in the complex fields of science and technology is unmatched among modern fiction writers. "Crichton has done his homework," says *Natural History* in reviewing his dinosaur books. "His dinosaurs are all plausible. His plot twists could happen. I know a bit about dinosaurs, so I know that Crichton takes care to be in the ballpark with his biology." [112] In 2000, in fact, pale-

Pulling Teeth

As a media celebrity, Crichton is constantly hounded for interviews. As an intensely private person, he seldom grants them. Occasionally, the need to boost publicity for a book or movie forces him to make a television appearance, which he hates. "I consider being on TV roughly the equivalent of having your teeth pulled," he admitted in a November 16, 1998, Barnes and Noble online interview.

Limited online chats with fans has been Crichton's most preferred method of handling interviews in recent years. When he does so, he is at times charming and at times impatient, especially with questions about his personal life. His answers are usually very brief; rarely does he go into any depth in his responses.

In 2000 Crichton became the namesake of a new dinosaur species, Bienosaurus crichtoni.

ontologists honored Crichton for his dinosaur work by naming a new species of dinosaur after him—the *Bienosaurus crichtoni.*

At the same time, no one can dispute that Crichton makes the most baffling technology readable or that he writes fast-paced, thrilling stories. Crichton's unique ability to float easily between the realistic world of science and technology, and the fantasy world of suspense and imagination, has made him wildly successful in both novels and films, not only in the United States but also throughout the world. His works have been translated into thirty languages, and eleven of them have been made into films.

In some ways, however, his unique skill has created problems for him with the critics. Intellectuals tend to dismiss him as a crude, popular entertainer just because his works are fun to read. Pop entertainment executives tend to see him as too intellectual just because his works include a wealth of information and explore contemporary issues. They bemoan the fact that Crichton has not capitalized on his *Jurassic Park* success by producing more of the same.

The critics' strongest case against Crichton remains the repeated charge that he is weak on character development. He admits that developing characters is not his strong point, but then neither is deep character development the point of his writing. There are times when Crichton presents himself as nothing but a humble, entertaining storyteller. "What I do is entertain people—that's all Dickens ever did, or R. L. Stevenson," [113] he has said.

But those who know Crichton say that he would prefer to be taken seriously for the ideas he presents in his books, not for his writing style. One of his editors, Sonny Mehta, remarks, "Michael is interested in issues. When Michael delivers a manuscript, we are all struck by how much we are made to think." [114]

An entertaining writer who makes people think. An intellectually brilliant writer who entertains people as he informs. Those descriptions may be as close as anyone comes to pinning a label on the elusive and unpredictable Dr. Crichton.

Notes

Introduction: Creator of the Technothriller

1. Quoted in Kevin S. Hile, ed., *Something About the Author,* vol. 88. Detroit: Gale Research, 1997, p. 56.
2. Quoted in Gregory Jaymes, "Meet Mister Wizard," *Time,* September 25, 1995, p. 62.
3. *Current Biography Yearbook: 1993,* "Michael Crichton." New York: H. H. Wilson, 1993, p. 140.
4. Nicholas Wade, "Methods and Madness," *New York Times Magazine,* December 5, 1993, p. 42.
5. Ron Givens, "Footnotes," *Newsweek,* July 20, 1987, p. 63.
6. Daniel Mendelsohn, "In Search of Lost Time," *New York Times Book Review,* November 21, 1999, p. 6.
7. Jesse Kornbluth, "Michael Crichton," *Architectural Digest,* April 1998, p. 323.

Chapter 1: Childhood Dreams

8. Quoted in Jaymes, "Meet Mister Wizard," p. 64.
9. Quoted in *Current Biography Yearbook,* "Michael Crichton," p. 140.
10. Quoted in Official Website of Michael Crichton, "*Time* On-Line Interview," September 22, 1995. www.crichton-official.com/ownwordsmain.htm.
11. Quoted in Official Website of Michael Crichton, "*Time* On-Line Interview," December, 1999. www.crichton-official.com/own wordsmain.htm.
12. Michael Crichton, *Travels.* New York: Alfred A. Knopf, 1988, p. 71.

13. Crichton, *Travels,* p. 74.

14. Quoted in Official Website of Michael Crichton, "CNN On-Line Interview." December 1999.www.crichton-official.com/own wordsmain.htm.

15. Quoted in Official Website of Michael Crichton, *"Book Reporter* Interview," December 2, 1999. www.crichton-official.com/own wordsmain.htm.

16. Quoted in *Current Biography Yearbook,* "Michael Crichton," p. 141.

17. Crichton, *Travels,* pp. 71–72.

18. Quoted in Official Website of Michael Crichton, "CNN On-Line Interview," November 1999. www.crichton-official.com/own wordsmain.htm.

19. Quoted in Official Website of Michael Crichton, *"Oprah* On-Line Interview," February 12, 1997. www.crichton-official.com/own wordsmain.htm.

20. Michael Crichton, speech to the American Association for the Advancement of Science, January 15, 1999. www.crichton-official.com./ownwordsmain.htm.

Chapter 2: Searching for a Career

21. Crichton, *Travels,* p. 4.

22. Crichton, *Travels,* p. 73.

23. Quoted in Official Website of Michael Crichton, *"Time* On-Line Interview."

24. Fred Rotondoro, *"A Case of Need," Best Seller,* August 15, 1968, p. 207.

25. Quoted in Ken Gross and Lorenzo Benet, "Michael Crichton Sends in the Clones," *People Weekly,* June 28, 1993, p. 130.

26. Quoted in Hile, *Something About the Author,* p. 58.

27. Crichton, *Travels,* p. 68.

28. Quoted in Official Website of Michael Crichton, *"ER* Interview," July 14, 1994. www.crichton-official.com/ownwords main.htm.

29. Quoted in Official Website of Michael Crichton, *"ER* Interview."

30. Quoted in Gregory Jaymes, "Pop Fiction's Prime Provocateur," *Time,* January 10, 1994, p. 52.

Chapter 3: Crichton and the Technothriller

31. *Current Biography Yearbook,* "Michael Crichton," p. 140.
32. M. B. Wergen, "Fiction," *Library Journal,* June 15, 1969, p. 2485.
33. Alex Comfort, *"The Andromeda Strain,"* *Bookworld,* June 8, 1969, p. 4.
34. Quoted in Jaymes, "Meet Mister Wizard," p. 63.
35. Quoted in Jaymes, "Pop Fiction's Prime Provocateur," p. 52.
36. *Current Biography Yearbook,* "Michael Crichton," p. 141.
37. R. A. Sokolov, "Patients' Dilemma," *Newsweek,* June 8, 1970, p. 89.
38. Henry Veit, "Mystery, Detectives, and Suspense," *Library Journal,* August 1972, p. 2653.
39. Quoted in the Official Website of Michael Crichton, *"Oprah On-Line Interview."*
40. Michael Crichton, *The Terminal Man.* New York: Alfred A. Knopf, 1972, p. xi.
41. Quoted in the Official Website of Michael Crichton, *"Oprah On-Line Interview."*
42. Tony Siaulys, *"The Terminal Man," Best Seller,* May 1, 1972, p. 52.
43. Quoted in *Current Biography Yearbook,* "Michael Crichton," p. 141.

Chapter 4: Searching for Identity

44. Crichton, *Travels,* p. 95.
45. Leonard Maltin, *Leonard Maltin's 2001 Movie and Video Guide.* New York: New American Library, 2001, p. 568.
46. Crichton, *Travels,* p. ix.
47. Peter S. Prescott, "Buzzers and Mutchers," *Newsweek,* June 23, 1975, p. 88.
48. Prescott, "Buzzers and Mutchers," p. 88.
49. Jack Sullivan, *"Eaters of the Dead," New York Times Book Review,* April 25, 1976, p. 22.
50. Quoted in Gross and Benet, "Michael Crichton Sends in the Clones," p. 130.
51. Donald Newlove, "Book Briefs," *Saturday Review,* November 1980, p. 72.

52. Peter S. Prescott, "Amy the Gorilla," *Newsweek,* December 15, 1980, p. 98.

53. Quoted in Jaymes, "Pop Fiction's Prime Provocateur," p. 54.

54. Maltin, *Leonard Maltin's 2001 Movie and Video Guide,* p. 83.

55. Pauline Kael, "The Current Cinema," *New Yorker,* November 9, 1981, p. 177.

56. Maltin, *Leonard Maltin's 2001 Movie and Video Guide,* p. 1199.

57. Quoted in *Current Biography Yearbook,* "Michael Crichton," p. 142.

Chapter 5: The Blockbuster

58. Robert Osborne, *Seventy Years of the Oscar.* New York: Abbeville, 1999, p. 243.

59. Givens, "Footnotes," p. 63.

60. Quoted in Official Website of Michael Crichton, "*Time* On-Line Interview."

61. Mick Martin and Marsha Potter, *Video Movie Guide.* New York: Ballantine Books, 1996, p. 829.

62. Quoted in Gross and Benet, "Michael Crichton Sends in the Clones," p. 130.

63. Quoted in Brian D. Johnson, "Myths in the Park," *Maclean's,* June 14, 1993, p. 43.

64. Quoted in Sharon Begley, "Here Come the Dinosaurs," *Newsweek,* June 14, 1993, p. 57.

65. Quoted in Begley, "Here Come the Dinosaurs," p. 57.

66. Quoted in Begley, "Here Come the Dinosaurs," p. 61.

67. Quoted in Gross and Benet, "Michael Crichton Sends in the Clones," p. 123.

68. Quoted in Johnson, "Myths in the Park," p. 43.

69. Quoted in Official Website of Michael Crichton, "*Time* On-Line Interview."

70. Crichton, speech to the American Association for the Advancement of Science.

71. Quoted in Official Website of Michael Crichton, "CNN On-Line Interview," December 1999.

72. Gary Jennings, "Pterrified by Pterodactyles," *New York Times Book Review,* November 11, 1990, p. 14.

73. Quoted in Jaymes, "Meet Mister Wizard," p. 62.

74. Quoted in Johnson, "Myths in the Park," p. 43.

75. Peter S. Prescott, "Big Birds! Leaping Lizards!" *Newsweek,* November 15, 1990, p. 69.

76. Quoted in *Current Biography Yearbook,* "Michael Crichton," p. 142.

77. Johnson, "Myths in the Park," p. 43.

78. Peter Travers, "JP," *Rolling Stone,* July 7, 1993, p. 120.

Chapter 6: The Media Celebrity

79. Quoted in Official Website of Michael Crichton, "*ER* Interview."

80. Quoted in Kornbluth, "Michael Crichton," p. 297.

81. Quoted in Kornbluth, "Michael Crichton," p. 323.

82. Quoted in Official Website of Michael Crichton, "CNN On-Line Interview," December 1999.

83. *Current Biography Yearbook,* "Michael Crichton," p. 142.

84. Robert Nathan, *"Rising Sun," New York Times Book Review,* February 9, 1992, p. 1.

85. Karl Taro Greenfield, "Return of the Yellow Peril," *Nation,* May 11, 1992, p. 636.

86. John Schwartz, "Whodunnit? The Japanese," *Newsweek,* February 17, 1992, p. 64.

87. John C. Tibbets and James M. Welsh, *The Encyclopedia of Novels into Film.* New York: Facts On File, 1998, p. xix.

88. Michael Coren, "Office Romance," *National Review,* February 21, 1994, p. 63.

89. Quoted in Malcolm Jones, "Moving Across Mediums," *Newsweek,* November 22, 1999, p. 94.

90. Quoted in Jaymes, "Pop Fiction's Prime Provocateur," p. 54.

91. Quoted in Official Website of Michael Crichton, "CNN On-Line Interview," December 1999.

92. Mark Annichiarico, *"The Lost World," Library Journal,* September 15, 1995, p. 91.

Chapter 7: Looking for New Challenges

93. Quoted in Official Website of Michael Crichton, "*ER* Interview."

94. Quoted in Official Website of Michael Crichton, "*Time* On-Line Interview."

95. Quoted in Official Website of Michael Crichton, "*ER* Interview."

96. Quoted in Official Website of Michael Crichton, "*Time* On-Line Interview."

97. Quoted in Official Website of Michael Crichton, "*Time* On-Line Interview."

98. Quoted in Jaymes, "Meet Mister Wizard," p. 66.

99. Quoted in Official Website of Michael Crichton, "CNN On-Line Interview," December 1999.

100. Quoted in Official Website of Michael Crichton, "Barnes and Noble Interview," November 16, 1999. www.crichton-official.com/ownwordsmain.htm.

101. Quoted in Jaymes, "Meet Mister Wizard," p. 66.

102. Quoted in Official Website of Michael Crichton, "Barnes and Noble Interview."

103. Quoted in Official Website of Michael Crichton, "*ER* Interview."

104. Quoted in Jaymes, "Meet Mister Wizard," p. 66.

105. Roy Olson, "Adult Fiction," *Booklist,* November 15, 1996, p. 548.

106. Quoted in Jones, "Moving Across Mediums," p. 94.

107. Mendelsohn, "In Search of Lost Time," p. 6.

108. Quoted in *Current Biography Yearbook,* "Michael Crichton," p. 143.

109. Quoted in Jones, "Moving Across Mediums," p. 94.

110. Quoted in Jaymes, "Meet Mister Wizard," p. 62.

111. Crichton, speech to the American Association for the Advancement of Science.

112. James Gorman, "Crichton's Jurassic Replay," *Natural History,* October 1995, p. 22.

113. Quoted in Hile, *Something About the Author,* p. 62.

114. Quoted in Jaymes, "Meet Mister Wizard," p. 63.

Important Dates in the Life of Michael Crichton

1942
John Michael Crichton is born in Chicago, Illinois; his family soon moves to New York.

1956
Sells first article, a travel story, to the *New York Times*.

1960
Accepted into Harvard University; enrolls as an English major.

1964
Graduates with a degree in anthropology; accepts offer to lecture in Europe.

1965
Begins Harvard Medical School; marries Joan Randam.

1966
First book, *Odds On,* is published under the pseudonym John Lange.

1968
A Case of Need, published under the pseudonym Jeffrey Hudson, wins the Edgar Award.

1969
Completes medical school; publishes *The Andromeda Strain,* his first best-seller; accepts a one-year fellowship at the Salk Institute for Biological Studies in California.

1970
Publishes *Five Patients,* a nonfiction work; separates from his wife and moves to Los Angeles.

1971

Publishes *Binary,* his most successful in the John Lange series; *The Andromeda Strain* is released as a major motion picture.

1972

Publishes *The Terminal Man;* his previous books, *A Case of Need* and *Dealing,* are made into films; directs his first film, a made-for-television version of *Binary* entitled *Pursuit.*

1973

Writes his first successful screenplay, *Extreme Close-Up;* directs his first feature film, *Westworld;* falls into a depression and begins to travel.

1974

The film version of *The Terminal Man* is released.

1975

The Great Train Robbery is published.

1976

Eaters of the Dead is published.

1977

Writes the screenplay for and directs the film *Coma.*

1979

The film version of *The Great Train Robbery,* which he wrote and directed, is released.

1980

Congo is published.

1985

After a period of writer's block, his creativity returns.

1987

Sphere is published; marries Anne-Marie Martin, his fourth wife.

1988

Travels is published; his daughter, Taylor, is born.

1990

Jurassic Park is published.

1992

The highly controversial *Rising Sun* is published.

1993

The film version of *Jurassic Park* becomes the best-selling film in history; *Rising Sun* is also made into a successful film.

1994

Disclosure is published; *ER* makes its debut and is an immediate television hit.

1995

The Lost World is published; it and *Disclosure* are made into major motion pictures.

1996

Airframe is published; Crichton and Anne-Marie cowrite the screenplay for the film *Twister.*

1999

Timeline is published; Crichton forms Timeline Studios to market his video games.

2000

Newly discovered dinosaur species *Bienosaurus crichtoni* is named after Crichton.

Works By Michael Crichton

Books

Odds On (1966, published under the pseudonym John Lange)
A Case of Need (1968, published under the pseudonym Jeffrey Hudson)
The Andromeda Strain (1969)
Five Patients (1970)
Binary (1971, John Lange)
The Terminal Man (1972)
The Great Train Robbery (1975)
Eaters of the Dead (1976)
Jasper Johns (1977)
Congo (1980)
Electronic Life: How to Think About Computers (1983)
Sphere (1987)
Travels (1988)
Jurassic Park (1990)
Rising Sun (1992)
Disclosure (1994)
The Lost World (1995)
Airframe (1996)
Timeline (1999)

Motion Picture Screenplays

Extreme Close-Up (1973)
Westworld (1973)
Coma (1977)
The Great Train Robbery (1978)
Looker (1981)
Runaway (1984)
Jurassic Park (1993)
Twister (1996)

For Further Reading

Michael Crichton, *The Andromeda Strain*. New York: Alfred A. Knopf, 1969. Crichton's first best-seller tells of frantic attempts to contain a deadly microbe from outer space.

————, *Congo*. New York: Alfred A. Knopf, 1980. Scientists use a signing gorilla to help them unravel a murder mystery deep in the jungles of Africa.

————, *Jurassic Park*. New York: Alfred A. Knopf, 1990. Crichton's most popular novel relates the tale of genetically engineered dinosaurs getting loose when a theme park's safety systems break down.

————, *The Lost World*. New York: Alfred A. Knopf, 1995. Crichton's only sequel, this revisits the theme of genetically engineered dinosaurs escaping their confines.

————, *Sphere*. New York: Alfred A. Knopf, 1987. A team of scientific experts are called in to investigate a strange alien craft at the bottom of the ocean, with terrifying results.

Works Consulted

Books

Michael Crichton, *The Terminal Man*. New York: Alfred A. Knopf, 1972. Crichton explores the dangers of tampering with the human brain in this story of an experimental medical procedure that leads to disastrous consequences.

——, *Travels*. New York: Alfred A. Knopf, 1988. This autobiography primarily covers two periods in Crichton's life: his medical school experience and his travels that began during his writing struggles in the mid 1970s.

Current Biography Yearbook: 1993. "Michael Crichton." New York: H.H. Wilson, 1993. Contains a fairly complete summary of Crichton's life and work.

Kevin S. Hile, ed., *Something About the Author*, vol. 88. Detroit: Gale Research, 1997. A similar summary of Crichton's life and work, with some illustration.

Leonard Maltin, *Leonard Maltin's 2001 Movie and Video Guide*. New York: New American Library, 2001. Another well-known film critic reviews films, including Crichton's.

Mick Martin and Marsha Potter, *Video Movie Guide*. New York: Ballantine Books, 1996. Film critics rate thousands of films, including those of Crichton.

Robert Osborne, *Seventy Years of the Oscar*. New York: Abbeville, 1999. A book of facts about the films and individuals who have won Oscar awards. Contains bare facts about Crichton and his contributions to television and video.

Julian Symons, *Conan Doyle: Portrait of an Artist.* New York: Mysterious, 1987. An interesting portrayal of the author of Sherlock Holmes uncovers striking similarities in the lives of Doyle and Crichton, who was a big fan of Doyle as a child.

John C. Tibbets and James M. Welsh, *The Encyclopedia of Novels into Film.* New York: Facts On File, 1998. Explains some of the background and infighting that has occurred in adapting novels, including Crichton's, into film.

Periodicals

Mark Annichiarico, *"The Lost World,"* *Library Journal,* September 15, 1995.

Sharon Begley, "Here Come the Dinosaurs," *Newsweek,* June 14, 1993.

Alex Comfort, *"The Andromeda Strain,"* *Bookworld,* June 8, 1969.

Michael Coren, "Office Romance," *National Review,* February 21, 1994.

Ron Givens, "Footnotes," *Newsweek,* July 20, 1987.

James Gorman, "Crichton's Jurassic Replay," *Natural History,* October 1995.

Karl Taro Greenfield, "Return of the Yellow Peril," *Nation,* May 11, 1992.

Ken Gross and Lorenzo Benet, "Michael Crichton Sends in the Clones," *People Weekly,* June 28, 1993.

Gregory Jaymes, "Meet Mister Wizard," *Time,* September 25, 1995.

———, "Pop Fiction's Prime Provocateur," *Time,* January 10, 1994.

Gary Jennings, "Pterrified of Pterodactyls," *New York Times Book Review,* November 11, 1990.

Brian D. Johnson, "Myths in the Park," *Maclean's,* June 14, 1993.

Malcolm Jones, "Moving Across Mediums," *Newsweek,* November 22, 1999.

Pauline Kael, "The Current Cinema," *New Yorker,* November 9, 1981.

Jesse Kornbluth, "Michael Crichton," *Architectural Digest,* April 1998.

John Lanchester, "Scare Tactics," *New Yorker,* December 16, 1996.

Daniel Mendelsohn, "In Search of Lost Time," *New York Times Book Review,* November 21, 1999.

Robert Nathan, *"Rising Sun,"* *New York Times Book Review,* February 9, 1992.

Donald Newlove, "Book Briefs," *Saturday Review,* November 1980.

Roy Olson, "Adult Fiction," *Booklist,* November 15, 1996.

Peter S. Prescott, "Amy the Gorilla," *Newsweek,* December 15, 1980.

———, "Big Birds! Leaping Lizards!" *Newsweek,* November 15, 1990.

———, "Buzzers and Mutchers," *Newsweek,* June 23, 1975.

Fred Rotondoro, *"A Case of Need,"* *Best Seller,* August 15, 1968.

John Schwartz, "Whodunnit? The Japanese," *Newsweek,* February 17, 1992.

Tony Siaulys, *"The Terminal Man,"* *Best Seller,* May 1, 1972.

R. A. Sokolov, "Patients' Dilemma," *Newsweek,* June 8, 1970.

Jack Sullivan, *"Eaters of the Dead,"* *New York Times Book Review,* April 25, 1976.

Peter Travers, "JP," *Rolling Stone,* July 7, 1993.

Henry Veit, "Mystery, Detectives, and Suspense," *Library Journal,* August 1972.

Nicholas Wade, "Methods and Madness," *New York Times Magazine,* December 5, 1993.

M. B. Wergen, "Fiction," *Library Journal,* June 15, 1969.

Internet Sources

John Callaham, "Michael Crichton Interview," Stomped, November 2, 2000. www.stomped.com/published/jcal973122121_1_1.html.

Michael Crichton, speech to the American Association for the Advancement of Science, January 15, 1999. www.crichton-official.com/ownwordsmain.htm.

Official Website of Michael Crichton, "Barnes and Noble Interview," November 16, 1999. www.crichton-official.com/ownwordsmain.htm.

———, *Book Reporter* Interview," December 2, 1999. www.crichton-official.com/ownwordsmain.htm.

———, "CNN On-Line Interview," November 1999. www.crichton-official.com/ownwordsmain.htm.

———, "CNN On-Line Interview," December 1999. www.crichton-official.com/ownwordsmain.htm.

———, "*ER* Interview," July 14, 1994. www.crichton-official.com/ownwordsmain.htm.

———, "*Oprah* On-Line Interview," February 12, 1997. www.crichton-official.com/ownwordsmain.htm.

———, "*Time* On-Line Interview," September 22, 1995. www.crichton-official.com/ownwordsmain.htm.

Index

Picture Credits

About the Author

Nathan Aaseng is an award-winning author of more than 160 non-fiction and fiction books for young readers, on a wide variety of subjects. Aaseng, from Eau Claire, Wisconsin, was a 1999 recipient of the Wisconsin Library Association's Notable Wisconsin Author Award.